DESIGN
SOCIAL
CHANGE

DESIGN SOCIAL CHANGE

Take Action, Work toward Equity,
and Challenge the Status Quo

Lesley-Ann Noel

Art by Che Lovelace

TEN SPEED PRESS
California | New York

HASSO PLATTNER
Institute of Design at Stanford

Contents

A Note
from the
d.school

At the Stanford d.school, *design* is a verb. It's an attitude to embody and a way to work. The core of that work is trying, to the best of one's abilities, to help things run more smoothly, delight more people, and ease more suffering. This holds true for you, too—whether design is your profession or simply a mindset you bring to life.

Founded in 2005 as a home for wayward thinkers, the d.school was a place where independent-minded people could gather, try out ideas, and make change. A lot has shifted in the decade or so since, but that original exuberant and resourceful attitude is as present today as it was then.

Our series of ten designer's guides is here to offer you the same inventiveness, insight, optimism, and perseverance that we champion at the d.school. Like a good tour guide, these handbooks will help you find your way through unknown territory and introduce you to some fundamental ideas that we hope will become cornerstones in your creative foundation.

Train your mind to see the present so you can shape the future in *Experiments in Reflection*. Go from idea to reality with *Make Possibilities Happen*.

And in this book, *Design Social Change*, take a good look at the causes and effects of oppression and find out how to unwind them to make this a more equitable world.

love,
the d.school

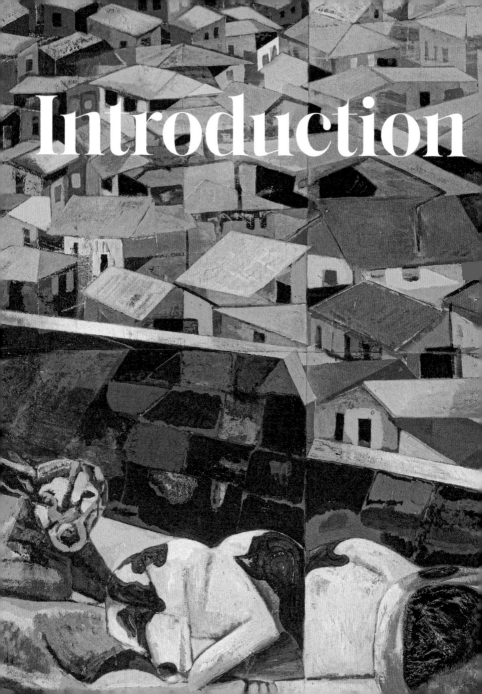

Introduction

f you find yourself thinking of cooking and food as you read this book, it is not accidental. This book began as a cookbook. Yes, you read that correctly. The seed for this book was a food analogy I've been using in the design classes that I've been teaching for several years: I ask my students, "Can we cook up change?" What if making a change that mattered was as easy as mastering ingredients and combining them the right way? What if we could just open our pantry, mix up some ingredients, and make some change? What ingredients and techniques do we need to learn to stir up change? Samin Nosrat's cookbook, *Salt, Fat, Acid, Heat* opens with the sentence, "Anyone can cook and make it delicious." I've been a product designer and design educator for more than twenty years, and that's how I feel about design and social change. Everyone can do this and make it good.

Of course, the ingredients for change are a bit different from those for my favorite Tobagonian dish, curried crab and dumplings. However, I find the process of designing the change you want to see in the world can be similar to following a recipe. It requires an understanding of ingredients—in this case those ingredients are things like anger about unfair treatment for you or others, joy about personal successes, and empathy for people who are oppressed. It requires a vision of the finished dish; a knowledge of the steps and methods; and, maybe most importantly, the courage and agency to change the process to suit your own style, what you have on hand, and each individual project. Your design recipes will turn out even more tasty if you add some special ingredients of your own.

This book is a place to start. It's about challenging the status quo. It is about learning to see what is not enough for you, especially if you're from an underrepresented group. It is about learning to see what is not enough for other groups in society around you. It's about identifying needs, making demands, and making change. And to do that, we'll use social justice concepts like building critical awareness, equity concepts like recognizing oppression, and design concepts like prototyping. This book is design-based, and design is action-based, so I hope you will create change through action. Throughout this book, you will be introduced to new concepts, theories, and methods that you can learn to combine to make the change you need.

The change that I am talking about is social change—the kind of change that led to the abolition of slavery in the Americas, the civil rights movement in the United States, the end of apartheid in South Africa, women's rights around the world, workers' rights, new labor laws in the twentieth century, and more. This book is about making the kind of change that will have a lasting impact on social practices. It's about the type of change that moves people beyond surviving to thriving. To achieve this, you need to know who you are and what motivates you as a changemaker, you need an awareness of the forces preventing you (and others) from thriving, and you need to make a conscious effort to "design out" these forces on individual and collective levels. In this book, the "Your Turn" activities will help you get to work with the concepts, and the "Take Note" sections will more deeply inform you on each topic. Throughout, you will find references to food, design, and personal stories that

I and other people have shared. You will also find art by Che Lovelace, an artist from Trinidad and my friend for many years. His art depicts scenes and people from Port of Spain in Trinidad, where I grew up; I hope these will help you reflect on the impact of social change.

The art in section 1 features a person looking reflectively off the canvas, setting the tone for reflecting on yourself and the world around you. The art in section 2 features two women looking at each other in a market, preparing you for collaborating with others in the real world. Finally, the art in section 3, depicts people and scenes from Port of Spain, and is representative of many places around the world that are ripe for social transformation. The city is rich with music and culture but is also affected by poverty and crime. In section 3, you are invited to consider how we create dreamspaces to carry places like the economically depressed urban communities of Port of Spain—like Belmont, where I lived for a decade—into the future.

Design is a powerful changemaker. Part of this power comes from the tools and process of design being able to adapt to fit your context, your style, and your community. You don't have to be a designer, and you don't have to accept tradition to use design for change. This book will show you how to get comfortable trying things out, exploring different methods, and using various approaches to design for equitable change. If it isn't perfect, it's okay; you can adapt and try again. What's important is taking that creative risk. Let's get to work stirring up change to create more equitable futures.

What's Wrong?

Building Critical Awareness

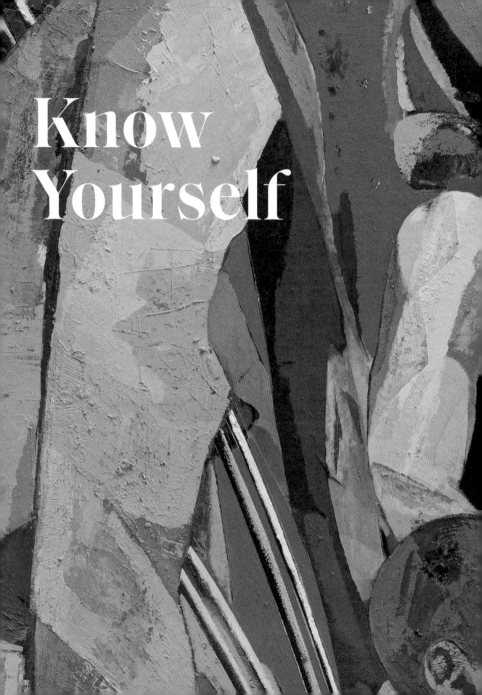

Know
Yourself

f I give you flour and water and ask you to make something by adding a few more ingredients, chances are that what you make will be different from what I would make. I am from Trinidad and Tobago, and with those base ingredients I might make either "bake," a type of bread with no yeast, or boiled dumplings. Depending on where you are from or the ingredients that you have on hand, you might make pizza, festival, chapatis, mandazis, sonhos, or even glue. You probably wouldn't say another person has made the wrong thing just because they make something different from you; intuitively you know that different people will make different things with flour and water. You might even be curious to know what other people will make, because you understand that your identity, your worldview, and past experiences—in other words, your positionality—will affect how you use the ingredients you have.

Declaring your positionality is a reflective practice of thinking about who you are, your identities, your social position, and how these affect your work. I learned the importance of declaring one's positionality while doing research as a graduate student. While there are some areas of research demand that you be objective and not bring your history and identity into the work you are doing, other areas of research recognize that this is impossible and invite you to reflect on who you are while you do the research. Qualitative researchers (that is, researchers who collect data using qualitative methods like interviews and observation) often create a positionality statement so that the person who reads the research can understand who made it and how their biases might show up.

We don't need to hide our identities from our work. Who we are shows up in everything we do, and that's not necessarily a bad thing. When we embrace our identities, our work becomes much richer as we bring these identities in.

Knowing who I am informs what I want to change.

Who Am I?

So, who am I? I am a Black woman from Trinidad and Tobago in the West Indies, less than ten miles from South America.

Both of my parents were first-generation college students, and both were from a generation in the Caribbean that saw massive social change. Despite these similarities, they had different upbringings.

My mother grew up in Jamaica in the 1940s and '50s, very proud, Black, and well educated. The value of education and its role in change, especially for girls, was emphasized in her family. My father grew up in Point Fortin in the south of the island of Trinidad, also in the 1940s and '50s. Point, as we call it in Trinidad, was bustling. Oil had been discovered in the 1930s. Immigrants from around the region found their way to Point to support the booming oil economy.

Both of my parents grew up on post-slavery, pre-Independence islands in the Caribbean. Even though slavery had ended in 1838, just about one hundred years before they were born, as children they listened to stories told by elders who remembered people who had been enslaved.

Both of my parents had experienced tremendous change by their early twenties. They both had to compete for scholarships to earn secondary education and university education. They both saw their colonial-ruled islands become independent territories in 1962. My parents witnessed thousands of people moving from abject poverty to the lower-middle and middle-middle classes over a few short decades. They also saw a radical change in access to many things for Black people, thanks to the Black Power movement and citizen protests against unfair or inequitable systems in the early 1970s. The social change that my parents witnessed led to new access to education and jobs, more upward mobility, and generally more power and visibility for people of African and Indian heritage in Trinidad and Tobago.

I was born in the 1970s in this restless environment and climate full of change. I am the product of the combined experiences of my parents. They laid a solid foundation that made me aware of and comfortable with my Blackness. They also made me aware of gender equity, as I was brought up in a gender-aware household, where my parents divided the housework. This upbringing has made me critical enough to recognize when something is not right. Their foundation also made me confident enough to call it out.

I left my parents' house in Trinidad and ended up in Curitiba, Brazil, where I was accepted into the industrial design program at the Universidade Federal do Paraná (UFPR). I had made a few stops along the way: I spent three months in Porto Alegre and a year in Salvador, Bahia, at Federal University of Bahia (UFBA). In Curitiba, I was exposed to wave after wave of social change in the six years that I lived there in my early to mid-twenties.

During my time in Brazil, I learned a new language and a new currency. I saw a president toppled and impeached for corruption. I saw the power of student protests and movements in toppling that president. I saw new economic stability after a change in the currency pushed millions of people into the middle class. With all of this, I became comfortable with change and learned that nothing had to be the way it was. I learned that access to education, economic stability, and the recognition of what is not enough can create massive social change. I learned that people have the power to stir up change.

My design practice has also made me comfortable with change. I studied graphic design, then industrial design, which led me to furniture design for several years. Now I operate primarily in the area of design for social innovation. Like many other designers in this evolving field, I've moved through various design specializations. I've worked with and taught both designers and nondesigners. This experience has helped me refine my own design language about change. Knowing who I am informs what I want to change.

My perspective as a mother makes me hyperaware of the need for change. As parents, we want better for our children.

My identity as a Black woman also makes me very aware of the change that is needed around us. I've never had to think about my Blackness before as much as I do in the United States. There isn't a day that I am not reminded about being Black, and this hit its peak with the collective anger at the murders of George Floyd, Breonna Taylor, and Ahmaud Arbery, and the anger at the way Amy Cooper confronted Christian Cooper in Central Park. My Blackness has changed in each of the places that I have lived. In Trinidad, though I was brought up in an Afro-conscious household, Blackness was not a liability. I was aware of my Blackness and aware of Black people's experiences of racism in other parts of the world, but I did not (or thought I did not) feel it in Trinidad and Tobago. In Brazil, I was a minority for the first time. Though I was the only Black student in my cohort, I still had the privilege of being a foreigner who spoke English. I was aware of the experience of my Black Brazilian friends, but mine was not the same. In Africa, my Black identity changed again. In Ghana and Mozambique, I felt at home and warmly welcomed as part of the family. In Kenya, Uganda, and Tanzania, I was more aware of my outsider status. My varied experiences and positionality as a person of African descent makes me know that I can demand more, no matter what place I am in.

Finally, based on my experience as a designer, I know that if we can envision it, we can make it. Or we can at least make something that gets us closer to our goals. And so, I dream of better and brighter futures, then work bit by bit to get closer to these futures I want.

The Process of Design and Change

Design for social change aims to transform societal structures, norms, and behaviors; for example, the civil rights movement sought to abolish institutional racism and segregation in the United States.

All design follows a process, and design for change begins earlier than you might think it does.

Prework and Planning. How do you begin? You pull together a team that includes people who are directly impacted by the issue you want to address, and you start researching. You can make the most change when you understand and address the issue from the viewpoint of the most marginalized groups, so work to ensure that barriers to participation are eliminated.

At the early stage, start with a base of equity considerations:

- Who will be on your team?

- How will you ensure that the issues are being driven by the most marginalized and affected groups?

- How will you reach people and compensate them for their involvement?

Understand the Issue: The Empathy Phase. This is where you dive deeper into the issue, ensuring that you understand it from the perspective of people who are closest to it. How do you do this? First, by making sure that your team includes people who understand the issue and that your team is having conversations, making observations, and reading what has been written on the matter from varying points of view. This stage could also include dreaming, with people who understand the issue, about new and better worlds.

Frame (and Reframe) the Issue. To create change, your team will need to consider the issue framed on different scales, from individual action to the community level. Take the time to frame and reframe the issue several different ways until you find the right problem frame. "Right" because it is the most impactful or achievable or meets other criteria for success as determined by the stakeholders who are most impacted.

Generate Ideas (aka, the Fun Part). Your team will create a portfolio of ideas that represent several ways in which the issue can be addressed. At this phase you will begin to see the possibility of collective impact: if the issue is addressed in different ways and at various scales, then many people can play a role in making change. Little by little the change that is needed can be achieved.

Test Your Ideas: The Prototype Phase. Select a few ideas to share with people to get feedback. As you make prototypes, you'll be able to elaborate on the ideas. When others interact with the ideas, you will get feedback that will make them stronger. It is important that the most marginalized people impacted by the issue are involved in both the prototyping and testing phases, including creating the criteria for success.

Reflect. Don't forget to pause to consider both the process and the outcomes. At one level, reflect on the people who participated in the process. Reflect on whether or not the marginalized perspectives were centered, and where marginalized people led the process. If this did not happen, reflect on how this will happen the next time. This is also a space to reflect on the impact of the solutions and how these can play a role in creating change. We can reflect on questions like these:

- How were students who are most impacted by an issue involved in a conversation about finding a solution?

- Did their concerns guide the drive for change?

- How did they lead the process?

You can apply this process to everything! I'm encouraging you to use it to create social change.

Who Are You?

In this chapter, I've shared a lot about myself. Now I want you to do the same and write a statement on your positionality. Writing a positionality statement can help you see who you are as you embark on your journey to stir up change. Sometimes we forget about some elements of our identity, or we focus on only certain things. Writing a positionality statement helps us to see our complexity.

Who are you? Think about the diversity that is represented within you. Push back against the world that asks you to fit in, and reflect on all the complexity that has made you. Here are some questions to consider in this reflection:

- Who had a big impact on you as a child? As an adult?

- What are some of the social changes that the people who are significant to you have experienced in their lives?

- What significant social changes have you experienced in your life?

- What are some of your many identities? Do any identities give you greater access to anything? Do any of these identities deny you access to anything?

- When has the world encouraged you to obscure or celebrate your identities?

- What is the one change that people with one of your oppressed identities need in order to thrive? For example, I am a mother, and one thing that mothers need to thrive is free or low-cost reliable childcare.

- What is one change you want to see in fifty years? Or before you die?

- What are some of the positive ingredients and experiences that have made you?

- How does the combination of ingredients that made you affect how you think about the world?

Reflect on your responses and write a description of who you are, what has made you who you are, and your vision for the future. Consider the complex combination of your identities with the identities of people who have had a significant impact on you.

This reflection is a form of positionality statement, in which you think of who you are in relation to the work that you do. This reflection on positionality can help you see your own agendas and possible biases. It can help you reflect on elements of your identity that you don't always see. This statement can help guide the work that you do. Come back to your positionality statement and reflect on it from time to time. Your positionality is also not fixed. It will change over time, as you age, as your abilities change, as your status changes. These changes will also impact the way you understand the world.

Positionality Wheel

The Positionality Wheel is another tool to prompt reflection about the way your worldview affects the work you do. Though I first made this activity for individual reflection on identity, it also works well with groups and helps teams to identify their own biases and gaps and how to balance their composition and ideas. This activity encourages all participants to reflect on facets of their identity ranging from more visible factors, like race, gender, and age, to less visible elements, such as ability, class, education, and even their languages.

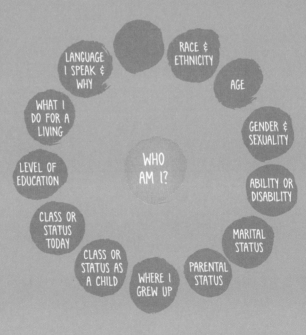

LANGUAGE I SPEAK & WHY

RACE & ETHNICITY

AGE

WHAT I DO FOR A LIVING

GENDER & SEXUALITY

LEVEL OF EDUCATION

WHO AM I?

ABILITY OR DISABILITY

CLASS OR STATUS TODAY

MARITAL STATUS

CLASS OR STATUS AS A CHILD

WHERE I GREW UP

PARENTAL STATUS

Ask everyone in the group to reflect on the twelve elements of their identities in the Positionality Wheel, then reflect individually and discuss as a group.

A disclaimer: Even the tools we build reflect the identities of the people who make them. I made the wheel based on what I deemed essential and what is supported by additional research. People have often asked me why I did not include identity markers that they feel are important, such as religion or political affiliation. I didn't include them because of the group I first made the wheel for and what I was focusing on. Please adapt this tool to suit the group with which you are working. Our template includes a blank circle for you to include elements of identity that should be included in your context; for example, religion, political affiliation, or even the high school that people attended, if relevant.

A second disclaimer: Reflections and discussions about identity can be uncomfortable. People should share only what they are comfortable sharing. The reflection on positionality can force people to reflect on unearned privileges they had not considered, or maybe even reflect on their identities that are not treated fairly in society. As you use the wheel, create space for that discomfort. Allow people space to talk, reflect, or even opt out of the activity.

Raising Critical Awareness

As I've mentioned, I love to cook (and the ritual of cooking). Before I begin to cook, I clear a space in my kitchen. Sometimes I put on an apron. Often I open my fridge. I think about the ingredients in my kitchen or pantry. Which fruits and vegetables are about to spoil and need to be used? If I'm going to cook meat, is it thawed? Even though I'm not quite ready to cook, I am preparing myself and my kitchen for the work that is about to happen. This is a wonderful metaphor for how to prepare yourself to do work that creates change. In creating change, you must first take a look around and ask: Where is change needed? What are the issues? Who's impacted? What's the environment? In short, you must build a critical awareness.

Paulo Freire was a Brazilian educator whose philosophies have deeply informed my way of thinking. From reading Freire, I learned that the oppressions we face do not define us. Through critical reflection we can first learn to see that oppression, then choose to take individual and collective actions against systemic injustices. Critical awareness makes us ask questions about why things are the way they are and how we can make them different. The process of building this critical awareness involves seeing, listening, and asking questions. It requires you to be in dialogue with the people and the world around you.

Building critical awareness will make you see the world with different eyes and not take things at face value. It makes you see more clearly where change is needed. You will also see that you have agency and can play a role in changing the circumstances.

Change is constant, which means what we want and need also changes. When we have a critical awareness, we can learn to shift our goals so they are always working for change.

The Three Stages of Critical Consciousness

Paulo Freire identified three stages of critical consciousness: naive, magical, and critical. With naive consciousness, we are aware of the problems that face us, but we merely act on the symptoms of these problems. With magical consciousness, we are silent and docile and accept injustices because it is the way of the world and we believe that it is our destiny or fate. With critical consciousness, we question the world around us and examine the root and structural causes of the issues that face us rather than accepting this is simply what has been dealt to us and beyond our power to change. Our goal is to work toward being in critical consciousness mode, in which we see the connections between our lives, the oppressions we face, and the society around us.

Take Note

What Do We Need to Change?

Social justice seeks equity in the distribution of wealth, opportunities, and privileges within a society and between individuals and their society. Ideas grow from tiny seeds to fringe movements to the mainstream and eventually bring about social change. This type of momentum has led to the end of slavery, the right to vote for women and people of color, and marriage rights for gay people. So, what are some things that need to change now? If I think of what my parents' generation went through to get a good education in times of segregation, then we have come a long way, but I want all of us to go even further—for me, my son, my friends in faraway places like Brazil and Tanzania, my friends' children, and people like my colleague who is a deaf designer. I'm still impatient and want more.

End White Supremacy and Racism. White supremacy affects everyone. It is the legacy of colonialism all around the world. In colonial times, Europeans believed they were superior to the people in and from the places they colonized. And this belief persists today. White supremacy and racism rob our society of humanity. When people experience discrimination based on their race at work or school, they are less likely to meet their full potential. Not all white people are racist, but all white people benefit from racism. Reverse racism, by the way, does not exist, because racism is tied to power. People of color can be continued

prejudiced against white people, but they do not have the power to benefit from their prejudices.

End Patriarchy. Patriarchy is how society supports the preferential advancement of men and the oppression of women. All men benefit from patriarchy. Men are assumed to be the breadwinners; they are overrepresented in leadership positions and are often paid higher wages than women. The dominance of the patriarchy is why women are expected to do more of the housework or take their husbands' surnames. Machismo and patriarchy prevent men from thriving when it prevents them from fully loving their sons and male friends. Patriarchy keeps everybody from leading a full life.

Queer Everything! Heterosexism is the presumption that people are heterosexual or that female-male attractions and relationships are the norm and therefore superior. Many of our institutions and systems, including our healthcare system, are heterosexist and do not adequately serve many people. Queering means challenging heteronormativity and identity binaries. As a design principle, queering creates greater equity for everyone, as we intentionally seek to challenge heteronormative products and services.

End Ableism. The old-fashioned way of responding to the needs of people with disabilities was to send them to institutions, such as schools and homes for the deaf and blind. Fortunately, we have reframed disability. Today we understand that often it is our society, more than the actual disabilities, that keeps people with disabilities from living full lives. While we can all benefit from programs, designs, and technologies that ensure greater access and participation for people with disabilities—think of curb cuts, screen readers, speech to text, and subtitles—we should not be seeking equity for people with disabilities or other groups at the margins just to benefit the mainstream. We need to seek better products and services for people and remove barriers to access because we want them to thrive.

Raising Your Critical Awareness

Freire used the term *critical consciousness*; I use the term *critical awareness* because it is easier for most people to understand. Critical awareness enables you to see the issues in the world around you. It helps you recognize your own agency and see how you can change the world. It also enables you to see the power and agency of others.

I challenge you to develop and fine tune your critical awareness. Question everything around you and don't take anything at face value. Only when you question the world around you can you begin to see where change is needed. Ask why! Don't accept the status quo! Your critical questions may annoy some, but they will help everyone move toward a better world.

How can you build your critical awareness? Start by answering the following questions to consider where you think change is needed in the world. Where are the friction points in your life due to certain elements of your identity? What is the change that would ease the friction?

I   Where are you in the consciousness stream?

- Naive consciousness—aware of the problems, but acting only on the symptoms of these problems

- Magical consciousness—silent and docile and accepting the injustices thrown at you because it is the way of the world

- Critical consciousness—questioning the world around you and examining the root and structural causes of the issues that you face rather than accepting these issues as merely what life has dealt out to you

2   What are some examples of inequity in the work you do or the world in which you live? What causes this inequity? What is the individual's role? What is society's role?

3   Think back to the activity in chapter 1, where you reflected on your positionality. How do you think your positionality might affect your critical awareness? Where might there be blind spots? Where might you be overstimulated?

4   Think about your day-to-day experiences. Where do you see examples of inequity? How does this inequity impact you?

5   Reflect on your own power and privilege. How do you benefit from inequalities? How are you disadvantaged because of them?

6   What are people doing to make change? Who is hacking inefficient systems around them to make things work? How can you work with them?

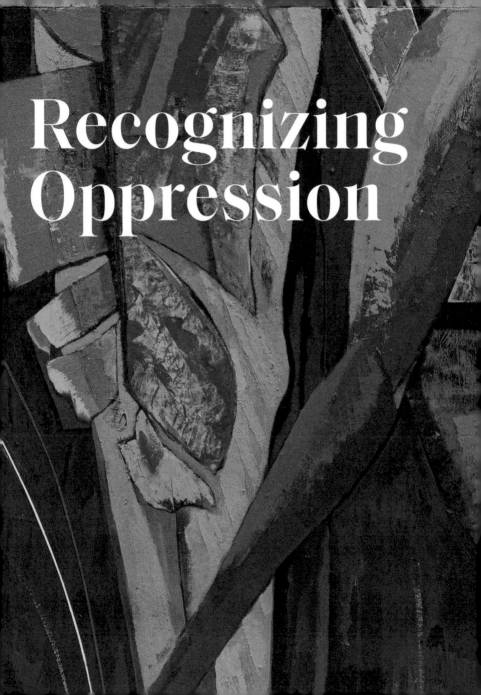

Recognizing Oppression

f building a critical awareness is like prepping to cook—putting on your apron and assessing your ingredients—then recognizing oppression is like the first step in the recipe. For me, that first step for all my savory dishes is always chopping onions and garlic—the base ingredients—even if I don't know exactly what I want to cook. As I chop the onions and garlic, I reflect on the food I am about to make. In designing change, you start by understanding oppression, even if you don't yet know what change you're working toward. This is where cooking up change begins: When you can see the forces that oppress, you can see how to make change.

The word *oppression* comes from the Latin word *opprimere,* which means to force down, weigh down, or suffocate. These are apt images for the oppressive forces that weigh down people and groups in society and prevent them from thriving. When you have developed the stance of critical awareness, you can then refine your skills to see where people (including yourself) are being pushed down and prevented from thriving. You can learn to see oppression more clearly.

Learning to see oppression humanizes and liberates us. And since our positionality changes throughout our lives, we also need to learn to see oppression so we don't step into the role of oppressors. For example, when people move into the middle classes, they sometimes lose sight of the oppressive forces that kept back the class they just left. So the ability to see oppression humanizes you as you try to make change. Merely wanting to have the same things as the oppressors—more power, money, status, and so on—does not create change. To achieve our collective liberation, we must each seek a better life for all—and for this, you need to build your critical awareness, see oppression, and learn to create the social action against oppression that leads to long-lasting change.

My parents grew up in worlds without white people. My mother says in Jamaica they weren't part of the world she lived in. She just never saw them. However, my father says his town in Trinidad had many white people, but the town was segregated. White folks lived on The Hill, while Black families, like his, lived down in the village. Black people and white people led very different lives in the same town in the Caribbean in the 1940s and '50s.

At one Christmas lunch, when we asked Dad about the different qualities of life for Black and white people, he said, "Well, we never actually questioned it. It just was the way things were."

Sometimes society is structured to prevent us from seeing the obstacles that prevent people from thriving. These obstacles may change from society to society.

The Different Levels of Oppression

Oppression is a complex phenomenon that operates simultaneously on interconnected yet distinct levels. The interplay between these different levels keeps people oppressed. Sometimes only one level of oppression is easily visible, but undoubtedly the other levels are also in play. Learn to look for all the levels of oppression that affect people so you can have a better understanding of the issues that they face.

In 2011, authors john a. powell, Connie Cagampang Heller, and Fayza Bundalli brought a systems-thinking approach to understanding oppression. Today, building on their work, many would agree there are four levels of oppression.

1 **Internalized oppression** is when an oppressed group believes the negative stereotypes that they hear about their own group and acts against their own group by discriminating against them.

2 **Interpersonal oppression** may be more familiar to most of us. It takes place between people, where people who are part of a dominant group discriminate against people from a minority group based on race, gender, age, class, ability status, and so on.

3 **Institutional oppression** is when the policies and systems of an organization discriminate against specific groups of people.

4 **Structural oppression** is when oppression and discrimination become ingrained in a society and are part of the culture. They are seen as "just the way things are."

A Note on Internalized Oppression

Internalized oppression happens when oppressed groups drink the Kool-Aid of the oppressors and use the oppressors' tools against themselves. For example, people judge and exclude people from their group because of their accents, hair, or social status according to cultural norms imposed by the dominant group. If you have an oppressed identity, take care of yourself and notice how your own internalized oppression might manifest itself. As a person educated in Latin America and the Caribbean, I sometimes doubted that I had a right to be in certain academic spaces. My internalized oppression caused me to doubt the power of the work that I was doing. Over time I've learned not to listen to my own self-doubts—and even when the doubt is still there, I won't hide my work. If you are from the group that is perceived as the dominant group, understand that the people you interact with may be struggling with their own internalized oppression and may need you to intentionally create space for them.

I challenge you to learn to see where change is needed. Where are people being held back by their own internalization of negative stereotypes, by other people, by institutional policies, and by society? Only when you can see this can you exclude from your design whatever prevents you from creating change.

The ability to recognize oppression and exclusion is a muscle that gets stronger over time. As this muscle becomes stronger, you will become more astute and see oppressions that you may not have noticed before. Racism and sexism may be the oppressions that we most readily identify. However, as your skill builds, you will learn to transfer this skill across different types of exclusion. You will start to see more clearly, for example, how gender binaries oppress and exclude or how written text may be inaccessible to some with different language or visual abilities.

Take Note

Five Types of Oppression-Related Injustices

Oppression is related to the domination of one group over another, social inequities, and differences in power. To better understand and identify oppression, it is useful to be able to see how it manifests as injustice in society. Psychologist Morton Deutsch identified **five oppression-related injustices** that make it easier to see oppression in action in the world around you.

1   **Distributive injustice** refers to the fairness of the distribution of resources, capital, benefits, and penalties. When we analyze the world around us, it is clear that resources and penalties are not distributed equally. Some groups receive more benefits while others receive more harm. For example, according to Time.com, in 2020, while 74 percent of white Americans owned their own homes, only 44 percent of Black Americans did. Many discriminatory factors—such as differential mortgage rates, redlining, and lack of multigenerational wealth negatively impact Black home ownership.

2   **Procedural injustice** refers to the fairness of processes. Will everyone get a fair process? Will processes favor one group of people over another? If, as a Black person, I get stopped on the side of the road by the police in the United States, will my Blackness automatically prevent

me from having a fair process? There are other situations where I know I will not get a fair process as a woman, a non-American, or a person with a foreign accent. Unfair processes are everywhere, and, in stirring up change, we can seek to identify these and strip them out of systems.

3   **Retributive injustice** refers to how we are judged for our wrongdoing. For example, if I was stopped by the police for going through a red light and my penalty is more severe than a white person's, an American's, or a man's, these *could be* examples of retributive injustice. If I face a greater penalty due to my Blackness, foreignness, or womanness, this *is* an example of retributive injustice. In stirring up change, we can look for examples of unequal penalties for wrongdoing and demand or ensure greater fairness and equality.

4   **Moral exclusion** happens when we think that people who are not part of our moral community, or people who do not share our moral philosophies, are not entitled to fair outcomes and treatment. Because of our allegiance to our moral community, we may not see this form of oppression happening around us. For example, we may think that undocumented people are not entitled to the same rights because they are not part of the moral group of citizens. Moral exclusion is, in fact, the justification behind xenophobia. It is the root of racism, genocide, slavery, colonialism, and other horrible eras in history. The idea that some groups are superior to others underpins

moral exclusion, and that superiority is used as a reason to oppress, push down, or exclude the other group.

5 **Cultural Imperialism** is when a dominant group imposes its culture, norms, values, and beliefs on another group. This dominant group values its culture over the culture of the group it has dominated. In design, the predominance of modernist and minimalist design worldwide could be seen as a form of cultural imperialism, since it displaces local design. When someone refers to "good design," they could be imposing their values and sensibility on other people and cultures. When groups of people are forced to speak the dominant language—for example, English instead of their native language, such as Spanish, or a dialect, such as African American Vernacular English (AAVE)—this could be a form of cultural imperialism.

To better understand
and identify oppression,
it is useful to be able
to see how it manifests
as injustice in society.

Finding Barriers

Sometimes in our design process, we want to solve an issue without understanding all the oppressive forces that are in play. In this activity you will look for the multiple levels of oppression that a person can face in one issue.

Have a conversation with someone you know about the barriers to their success or the success of a family member. How would they define their success and thriving? What would help them to lead happier lives? What are the things that are holding them back? Are they acting against the oppressions that they face?

As you listen to what is holding them back, determine on which level of oppression the barriers are located: internalized, interpersonal, institutional, or structural. These levels are probably interconnected. When we don't see the full picture, we may assume that the barriers are internal. Expand your thinking about what the person has told you. Dig deeper and find the interconnected barriers on each level.

For example, you had a conversation with Elena, who said:

> *My barrier to success is a better job. A better job would lead to more money and that would help me have a better life. If I could go back to school, I could become qualified to get a new job, but I can't. I just had a baby and have no childcare and I can't go back to school anyway. So I'm stuck.*

Using the four levels of oppression, we can identify the barriers that Elena is facing:

Internalized oppression	Interpersonal oppression	Institutional oppression	Structural oppression
Elena may think she does not have the intellectual capacity to apply for certain jobs or to get additional education to become qualified for different jobs.	Elena is older than the other students and is a parent. Teachers and other students treat her differently and are condescending. Her relationships with others and the way others see her could prevent her from thriving as she goes back to school.	Elena would like to go back to school, but because of her age, she is prevented from enrolling in the program. Classes are also scheduled at times that are incompatible with parenting. The policies at the school she wants to go to will prevent her from going back.	In some countries, girls who have become pregnant are not allowed to finish school. Girls who are mothers are prevented from having access to education. This is a form of structural oppression, since it is not at the level of the institution, but at a higher level across institutions.

Have a conversation with someone in your life and complete the activity above, showing what is holding the person back and the barriers on internalized, interpersonal, institutional, and structural levels.

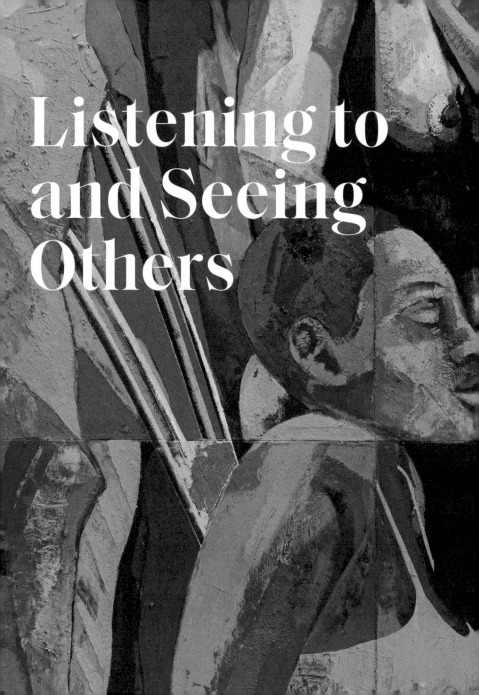

Listening to and Seeing Others

After you have gained a critical awareness of the world and have started to recognize oppression, it's important to learn to pay attention to details around you. Learning to connect with people, listen to them, and see their concerns will give you a deeper understanding of the issues surrounding the change you want to make.

There is always a bigger picture of both oppressing and liberating forces around every person and issue.

Learning to See

Sometimes we look only at what's right in front of us, but we must also look at the space around it. This is a common lesson in art and design classes: It's important to draw both the object and the negative space around it. The same is true when we're looking at an issue. What are all the factors and systems surrounding the phenomenon that we want to change? Who are the people at the heart of this issue—the oppressors and the oppressed? (Most people move between the roles of oppressor and oppressed throughout their lives.) We need to look at each side and ask: What trauma has made the person who they are? What trauma holds them back in life? What joys buoyed their childhood? There is always a bigger picture of both oppressing and liberating forces around every person and issue. We must learn to see them. Here are some tips to help you see people:

- Make eye contact.

- Be present and not distracted by devices and technology.

- Read their body language and responses to you and the world around them.

- Examine power. Who has it? Why? And how? What would make them more powerful or powerless?

- Recognize your own lenses and biases as you see others.

Learning to Listen

To create change in a culture where people do not slow down to listen to each other, it's important to learn to stop and pay attention. Listen to people when they talk. What are the details of their conversation? Listen to what they are saying when they are not saying anything.

As we grow up, our talking skills are heralded. We get awarded great grades for doing presentations, but perhaps we aren't as well rewarded for listening or connecting.

In secondary school, I studied French. My French teachers—Madame Bartholomew, Madame Hunte, and Mademoiselle Garcia—taught us to pay attention to tiny details to improve our accents and respond to questions. They would bring us real sound clips from French or Martinican radio and TV stations, and we learned to pay attention to find the hidden details in the recordings. If you have ever had to learn a language, recall how you had to pay attention to sounds and how you formed your mouth to speak. You learned through looking and listening and practicing. You can bring that attention into your everyday life. Listen to the details of conversations that you have. How do people express joy, sadness, happiness—the whole gamut of emotions? How do people ask for help without asking? How do people show love?

In a recent Caribbean meme, the main character was asked how they said "I love you" in their local dialect. The character struggled and struggled to mouth the words.

After a marked silence, he said, "I bring food for you." I squealed with laughter as I watched the video because it was so true. Some people can't say they love you, but they will show their love through gestures like cooking and making sure we, the people they love, are fed. How many people do you know who can't say that they love you but find different ways to convey their feelings?

Part of learning to listen is learning to identify the different ways in which people communicate their thoughts and feelings. Sometimes people tell us important things even though they might not use the words we expect—or they might not use words at all. If people can't tell us clearly how they feel and what they need, then the skill of listening and connecting is vital to understanding what they need to thrive. Listening reduces misunderstandings and builds trust and relationships. In learning to listen, we can begin to understand issues more deeply and empathize with others.

Oppression is the phenomenon of people being pushed down. To be able to identify those who are oppressed, we need to listen to the stories and voices of oppressed people. This is particularly important because in a culture of oppression, the viewpoints of people who are oppressed are always questioned. Distrust is a tool of the oppressor, and we must learn to develop trust with the oppressed—to hear their stories and connect with them as humans. Where do people feel marginalized, exploited, dominated (culturally or otherwise), powerless? We need to learn to listen when people tell us how they are being pushed down, even if they communicate this in unexpected ways.

Poor listening skills can have many causes, such as being distracted by other people, tasks, activities, and priorities. Practicing good listening means intentionally removing other distractions. You may have to use tools to help you focus, such as a pencil and a notebook to take notes. You may have to repeat what someone said to you to understand and prove that you were listening. Here are some tips to help you listen to people:

- Listen without interrupting.

- Don't focus on what you're going to say next.

- Leave space for a pause after they have finished speaking, in case they'd like to say more.

- Use prompts and inviting words like "tell me more" to get them to open up.

- Use open-ended questions instead of yes or no questions to better understand their issues.

- Suspend your views, interpretations, and opinions while you are listening.

Empathy + Design

In design we talk about empathy a lot. Empathy is the deep awareness of the experience of others. Empathy evolved as a survival mechanism to fast-track our understanding of the world. For example, millions of years ago if one person ate food that killed them, our empathetic response would teach us to not do the same thing. Of course this is an oversimplification of the development of empathy, but you get the idea.

Empathy is often considered one of the first phases of the design process, when we attempt to understand the experience of people we are designing for. To understand the experiences of others, we use many design research methods (some borrowed from anthropology), such as observation and interviews.

The concept of empathy in design is complicated though. Irrespective of how much research we do, there is a limit to how far we can understand the experience of others. So while we do use empathy to understand others' experiences in the design process, there are limits to how much we can understand experiences that we have never had. Participatory design advocate Victor Udoewa recommends a strategy to move beyond empathy. We cannot really understand experiences we have not had, so he proposes that people who *have* had the experience join the design team. When there are people with lived experiences of the issue on the team, other members will not have to rely solely on imagining that experience.

Learning to See Others

Every issue is more complex than we first think it is. Structural factors provide advantages for some people and marginalize or present disadvantages for others. There are individual factors, which designers are often trained to understand by using the skills of empathy. In learning to see others, we need to learn how to take in the complexity of their lives and the factors we want to change.

Think about a topic you want to address. What are the issues in the negative space surrounding the problem you want to focus on? For example, you may be thinking of a social issue like that of people without housing. You ask, "Why are people unhoused?" Looking beyond the individual who is unhoused, can you see what invisible issues impact this issue? What factors prevent the unhoused from having a more stable living arrangement? Is it the lack of affordable housing, poverty, an economic or medical crisis, divorce?

What is the weather in that city? You are more likely to find unhoused people in a city with good weather than bad, so Buffalo, New York, is likely to have fewer unhoused people than Los Angeles. What factors are likely to draw the person to that place or keep them there?

Push yourself to see the many complex factors around the issue that frame it in the way we generally see it. Think back to the four types of oppression: internalized, interpersonal, institutional, and structural. As you focus on the issues that are pushing each of us down, reflect on which forms of oppression these issues are related to.

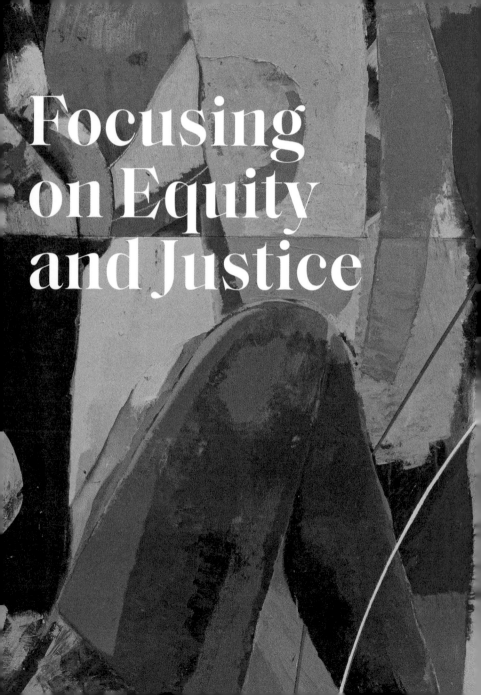

Focusing on Equity and Justice

You've been introduced to building a practice of being more critically aware, recognizing oppression, and spending time listening to and seeing others. Now it's time to focus on designing injustice *out of* and designing equity *into* everything you do.

Equity is a word we often hear these days. It refers to fairness and justice. As a child, I was trained to think that things were fair if everyone got the same. Early on in life, we learn it's important to treat people equally. Sometimes, however, it's necessary to distinguish equity from equality. Whereas equality generally means providing the same to all, equity means recognizing that we do not all start at the same place and therefore have different needs. Equity is focused on ensuring that people have equal outcomes, even if they need different inputs.

When working toward equity, we need to hold onto our critical awareness so we can see the obstacles that block our progress. There are historical, political, economic, and cultural obstacles in society. While equality and equity are both grounded in the same concept of fairness, one concept sees all of us as the same and is value-neutral, whereas the other concept recognizes difference. Equity recognizes the unique lived experience of each individual with regard to their historical, political, and economic context. So if we want equitable outcomes, we must begin by acknowledging that we are not all the same and that different obstacles and barriers prevent us from success. A third element of this discussion is a variation of the concept of equality that recognizes that individuals within the same category should be treated the same but also recognizes that there may be differences across categories. The South African constitution is based on this type of equality, as it seeks to right decades of apartheid through differential treatment for different groups within its population.

This difference in perspective leads to different kinds of questions, asking *How might we give people what they need to thrive?* rather than *How might we give everyone the same tools?* For example, instead of designing and creating programs about distributing textbooks or computers to all students, someone in education seeking to ensure the opportunity for equal outcomes for all students might create programs that offer more face-to-face tutoring rather than just distributing textbooks. Some students may need different types of support to thrive.

Here's another example. My friend is looking forward to retirement in the United Kingdom, where she is a citizen. In some parts of the country, the life expectancy is in the eighties and as high as the nineties. However, life expectancy in her part of the country is lower than the retirement age of sixty-six. She is sixty-one and worries that she won't have equitable access to a post-retirement life and pension simply because of where she was born and has lived her life.

An equitable approach to retirement could mean that the retirement age would be adjusted so that people from the working class and people in poor health, with prison records, and from other sections of the population with considerably lower life expectancies would be able to receive a pension for a reasonable length of time. Another approach to this problem would require understanding about what is causing the difference in life spans between the neighborhoods with high life expectancy and those with low life expectancy, then working on programs to increase the life expectancy of the latter group.

My friend put it this way:

> That's not actually any version of equality. What I want is equity, where people actually have a chance to live lives and get a pension for a reasonable amount of time. In many communities, people never make it to that age. People who've been in prison, for example, tend to die in their fifties. They're not going to make it to pension age when they get out.

To better understand gaps, inequity, and people's needs, you have to learn more about their journeys, struggles, and joys. You need to find out what makes them tick, what will make them thrive. To do this, you need lots of empathy for the stakeholders, your teammates, and yourself.

Justice is a concept in ethics and law that means fair, equal, and balanced treatment for everyone. And similarly to oppression, there are different categories:

- **Social justice** is the view that everyone deserves equal economic, political, and social rights and opportunities.

- **Racial justice** is the systematic fair treatment of all races, resulting in equitable opportunities and outcomes for all.

- **Climate justice** relates to concerns about the inequitable outcomes for different people and places associated with vulnerability to climate impacts and the fairness of policy and practice responses to address climate change and its consequences.

Injustice is the denial of justice. When you see inequity and injustice both in the world around you and in the work that you do, you must ask yourself what you can do to remedy it.

To transform society and create change, you sometimes need to treat people differently. You sometimes need to use "fair discrimination," whereby you give preferential treatment to the groups that need more support to be able to thrive, making up for years of systemic injustice. You do this, for example, through affirmative action laws, intentional allocation of resources to underserved communities, and doing businesses with minority business owners. In seeking to create equity, you have to be discriminatory and reallocate resources to those who did not traditionally have access. By paying attention to gaps across differences, you will eventually achieve a level of sameness that is better for everyone. Achieving equity requires recognition that because some people have been denied access and benefits, they deserve greater accommodations in order to achieve equity and both bold goals and bold steps to reach them.

Your challenge, as you design products and services, is to find where the need is greatest. Who needs the leg up to get to equal outcomes? What systems and practices keep people back, and how can you design hurdles to equity out of your goods and services? Where is the need? Is it among people with children? First-generation homeowners? People within a specific age group? In your work, you'll need to play the role of super-sleuth or detective and find inequities that are baked into products, services, and systems, then design them out.

A Checklist for Equity in the Design Process

Sometimes in the design process you'll need some reminders to help ensure that you keep equity in focus. For several years I've been asking different collaborators what prompts would help them focus on equity at each stage of the design process. I've compiled a collection of prompt questions from community collaborators, city officials, students, and colleagues. I asked people to focus on equity throughout the design process intentionally. The question bank can be used for reflection to help ensure that equity is top of mind throughout the process.

The following list presents questions for equity at every stage of the design process.

These aren't the only possible prompts to ensure equity-centered design. They might not be the correct questions for your design work. Consider this list an invitation for you to create your own list and questions for reflection.

As you use the question bank, consider the following:

- Which of these questions are relevant to your process?

- What additional questions would you ask?

- How can you center equity in your work?

Prework and Planning

- Are people from historically marginalized communities part of the project team or advisors to the project team?

- How will collaborators be compensated for their time?

Understand the Issue: The Empathy Phase

- Who is historically excluded from conversations about this problem? What are these people's concerns? Where are they in this design process?

- How will you connect with other partners and collaborators in the problem space?

Frame (and Reframe) the Issue

- Who defined the problem or issue, and why?

- What do the main stakeholders want to focus on? Have we gathered information directly from their point of view?

- Has the issue been framed around the wants and needs of the stakeholders at the margins?

- Can the issue be framed around replacing harmful systems rather than incremental reform?

- How does addressing this problem dismantle systems of oppression?

Generate Ideas

- Are the most impacted stakeholders involved in the solution-finding process, either through codesign or by giving regular feedback on the designs?

- Do the solutions intentionally aim to change systems of oppression?

- What are the stakeholders already doing as a workaround to manage the issue? How can the intervention amplify the work that is already being done?

- Instead of a solution for individuals, what version of the solution will build community relationships?

Test Your Ideas: The Prototype Phase

- Are the most impacted stakeholders involved in the making and testing process through various iterations of testing?

- What is a community-owned, worker-owned, or another collective version of the proposed solution?

- What is a low-cost and low-tech version of the proposed solution?

- Who has been involved in making the prototype?

- Have the most impacted stakeholders been engaged in creating criteria for success?

- Have the most impacted stakeholders given their feedback on the proposed solutions?

Reflect

- How does the solution impact systems of oppression?

- How has the solution contributed to supporting the stakeholders to lead full and healthy lives?

- Can the stakeholders take ownership of the work? How can they implement it without your further involvement?

- What more could be done to replace the harmful systems rather than incrementally reform them?

What questions would you add to this list?

What Does It Feel Like?

Deepening Emotional Intelligence

Anger
and Joy

As you focus on creating social change, a wide range of emotions will arise. You may feel sadness or anger as you reflect on what has been denied to you or others. You may be surprised as you develop different understandings of an issue. You may experience joy through the relationships you form as you work with others, and anger at the roadblocks you hit along the way.

Anger and joy can seem like polar opposites, but these two emotions remind us of the wide range that people can feel as they respond to an issue. Leaning into both anger and joy will lay the foundation for you to understand and explore issues through the lens of various emotions, including surprise, fear, excitement, pain, and worry. We need emotions in design work in general and in design for social change in particular because they help identify the issues that are meaningful to us and the people we work with. Emotions also make it easier to communicate and bond with others. When we don't bring our emotions into the design process, we miss vital information about the world around us. We miss cues that could lead us to make better decisions. It becomes more difficult to bond with others, making the collaboration process more difficult. Emotions are always present in our work, and we should get good at working with them.

Anger

"Do you want to make these children angry?" A school administrator once asked me this question as I showed her my draft elementary school design curriculum to promote critical consciousness. She was worried about how the school would control the angry children. "What will we do if these children become angry?" she asked. The administrator was not wrong. In fact, I wanted the children to ask questions about what was and what wasn't good enough for them, and this could be interpreted as wanting to make them dissatisfied or angry. I wanted them to see that even though they were children from a rural school and were expected just to take what they could get, they could have more.

Anger is a key ingredient in stirring up change. Anger is a natural and primitive emotion meant to protect us from threats. When we are angry, we are responding to some form of threat to our well-being. Anger is a natural response to this threat. Anger creates energy and movement. It fuels action. It prompts us to find solutions to what is bothering us. When we combine our anger with that of others who are also passionate about causes, movements are created. In that solidarity, it is possible to make even more significant change. Rather than bottling in your anger and struggling on your own, go find other people who are passionate about the same causes and who can work with you to make a dent in the problem you are addressing.

Anger can be frightening, but dissatisfaction is needed to prompt change. It is anger and conflict that spark social change! So, while it may be tempting to tell yourself and others to calm down, there is power in learning to channel your anger into positive change.

I once received some excellent advice from an older professor. I was walking around so angry that steam was escaping from my ears, and the dear gentleman pulled me aside and said, "It's okay to be angry. But take that anger and turn it into something productive. Go write a paper. Turn it into a book." The advice catapulted my career as I channeled dissatisfaction or anger into creative outputs designed to change whatever I was reacting to.

Anger brings a much-needed spice to the work that we do. It is a bitter flavor that adds more complexity to the taste of change. Add a dash of anger or rage to some of what you do! In her book *Seven Necessary Sins for Women and Girls,* Mona Eltahawy says that she leaned into her anger and wrote her book while she was filled with rage. Eltahawy also says anger that is not expressed becomes internalized as sadness. So instead of bottling up her anger about sexual assault, sexism, and patriarchy, she used the feelings to fuel her writings, which turned into an instruction manual for other women about smashing the patriarchy.

Use your anger to challenge the status quo and to help us see some of the normalized oppression. Challenge people to do better. Channel your anger into doing good work and making the world a better place.

Take Note

Strategies for Thriving in the Face of Hostility

In making change, we can encounter anger from all sides: anger at the inequity that pushes us to make change and anger from those we're asking to change. Resistance to change can create a hostile environment. As someone who is making the change, you must understand how to thrive despite the negativity and anger of others.

You can respond to hostility and negativity using a variety of strategies. Some are inward-facing, some push you into action, and some are about building relationships. Other approaches focus on protection and defense or distraction or diffusion.

Some **inward-facing strategies** against hostility include building confidence in yourself. You know that your focus on making change will put you on the right side of history, because historically, despite whatever despair you might feel about equity, society trends toward becoming more equitable rather than less. Believe in your inner strength. Another inward strategy is finding your inner peace through an activity like meditation or pursuing spirituality. Reflection is another inward strategy that helps you to better understand a situation or the viewpoint of hostile people.

One **action strategy** against hostility is preparing to respond to negative feedback. Gather your counterarguments. Let the other person's anger make you sharper.

A **relationship-based resilience strategy** to counter the anger and negativity of others may include knowing that you're not alone and building communities of support. Mentors can also help see you through your struggles by offering both guidance and encouragement.

Distraction or defusion strategies balance the anger and hostility by providing momentary escapes. These could be through hobbies and fun activities like sport or exercise, or relaxing and coping mechanisms such as meditative, or reflective creative practice like art, music, and dance. Games and comedy may make you laugh and forget the hostility of others. These strategies energize you, so you're stronger when you come back to the struggle.

Take the long view. You can take comfort that your cause that seems fringe now will eventually become more mainstream, even though it may not seem like it at the moment.

Joy

On the flip side, we also need joy—that feeling of great pleasure and happiness—to create change.

Although exposing pain points and hardship can lead to change, in my own design process I no longer want to focus only on pain. Now I acknowledge the complicated power dynamics of merely observing the pain and suffering created by various forms of oppression. I notice the complexity of looking at other people's pain yet not seeing my own of looking at other people's pain and not seeing their happiness as well or of thinking that only people like me can be happy. It is necessary to understand people's happiness, joy, ecstasy, and other positive emotions to disrupt the power differentials and learn to see the complexity of the people we work with.

It's also important to note that joyful movements attract people and motivate them to stay involved. Look for ways to make change through creating joyful moments in social movements, whether through satisfying relationships with other changemakers, through building community, or through food, dance, fellowship, festivities, and more.

Joy can be an antidote to one of the pitfalls of design for social change: a hyperfocus on the problems, which can lead to both a limited and deficit-centric view of the issues and the people the designer is attempting to serve and an unbalanced power dynamic, where the designer feels superior to those they are serving. To balance this hyperfocus on the problems, one semester, early in the COVID-19 pandemic, I gave my students the assignment to intentionally focus on the joy of the people they interviewed for class. If they could not describe joy from the interviewees' point of view, the assignment was incomplete. When we focused on joy, the student proposals lost much of the patronizing urge to fix everything that can sometimes be found in design for social innovation, which involves the use of design to promote new solutions to social issues. When the student proposals also focused on the participants' joy, they came up with a wide range of solutions that aimed to ensure and perpetuate the participants' joy while also creating access to good health and well-being, which was the brief for the class. Their ideas included food trucks, block parties, community gardens, recipe-sharing platforms, and more—a collection of much livelier and richer ideas than simply solving for the problems.

One way to access joy is through play. Play can relieve stress, promote learning, and foster connections between people and the world around them. It also teaches cooperation with others and can heal emotional wounds. Could play be a design principle in your work?

In your work in creating change, learn how to balance anger with joy. Black and Latinx stories aren't only about suffering. We can also create design projects around hopes, imagination, festivals, futures, happiness, building community. As a designer and changemaker, you don't have to focus on suffering and sadness. Find joy in what you do. Discover what brings joy to other people. Design ways of moving out of anger and moving into spaces of joy where people can thrive. Explore alternative framings to the issues you want to focus on, and keep in mind that joy, happiness, and positivity are legitimate frames for your work. What brings joy to you and the people you collaborate with? Do your proposed solutions spark joy? As others have said before me, your joy is an act of resistance and can also be a form of protest. Choose to design a joy-filled and satisfying life.

Exploring Emotions

I was introduced to the Feeling Wheel, which was created by the late Dr. Gloria Willcox, by my friends, Jabari Brown and Dr. Jeanne Firth, who are great diversity, equity, and inclusion (DEI) facilitators.

Dr. Willcox created the Feeling Wheel to expand people's awareness of their emotions and to help them categorize these emotions. The wheel shows that despite the complexity of the words we use, many of our feelings can be reduced to six emotions: sad, mad, scared, peaceful, powerful, and joyful. In my design research, the Feeling Wheel helps me understand and name the emotions that people experience. I also use the Feeling Wheel, and the more recent Emotion Wheel by Abby VanMuijen (shown on page 67), to prod myself to ask deeper questions that uncover a wide range of emotions about a person's experience.

For us as designers, pain points, anger, and negative feelings are easy to respond to. It's a bigger challenge to use other emotions—such as joy, peace, fear, and power—as starting points for a design. Focusing on maintaining positive emotions such as joy, peacefulness,

continued

and powerfulness, or mitigating and managing emotions that are perceived as negative such as anger, sadness, or fear can dramatically change design outcomes.

Interview someone you know about the issue you want to change. Where do people feel peaceful, joyful, and powerful regarding this issue? How can you maintain these good feelings through design? You can use the Feeling Wheel or the Emotion Wheel (facing page) to simplify the emotions that people describe. For example, if your interviewee talks about being fascinated by something, you can use the wheel to see that this is a joyful experience.

Outer ring (clockwise from top):
GUILT • DIGNITY • LIBERATION • INTUITION • COURAGE • RAGE • REACTIVITY • GRIEF • ISOLATION • VULNERABILITY • SHAME

Center segments: JOY, GENIUS, ANGER, SAD, FEAR, DISGUST

JOY (top): GRATEFUL, PLEASURE, BELONGING, LOVE, SATISFIED, RELIEF, EASE, NOTICED, CALM, PRESENT, CONNECTED, INTEGRITY, SAFETY, CARE, AWE

GENIUS / Anger side: SILLY, CURIOUS, WONDER, BRAVE, ACCEPTANCE, ALIVE, INTERESTED, LIKE MYSELF, UNIQUE, FOCUSED, CREATIVE, CONFIDENT, CHALLENGED, IN FLOW, AGENCY, UNAFRAID, MOTIVATED

ANGER: PROTECTIVE, IRRITATED, TENSE, SKEPTICAL, DEFENSIVE, MAD, AGGRESSIVE, RESENTFUL, DISAPPOINTED, LOYAL, FRUSTRATED, RESISTANT, DISTRUST, CLOSED OFF, ENVIOUS, ACTIVATED, HATEFUL, HURT, DEPRESSED

SAD: DISCONNECTED, LOSS, TIRED, UNMOTIVATED, BORED, LONELY, LOST, NUMB, BURNT OUT, EXHAUSTED, HEARTBROKEN, ISOLATED, DIRECTIONLESS

FEAR: VULNERABLE, INSECURE, WORRIED, STRESSED, DISORIENTED, UNSAFE, BUSY, INSIGNIFICANT, INTIMIDATED, DREAD, ANXIOUS, FIXATED, SOMETHING'S WRONG, PANIC, OVERWHELMED, IMPOSTER SYNDROME

DISGUST: ASHAMED, HUMILIATED, JUDGMENTAL, AVERSION, COMPLICIT, NAUSEOUS, AWFUL, UNSETTLED, AVOIDANCE, SELF-CONSCIOUS, UNCOMFORTABLE, GUILT, PITY, JEALOUS, EMBARRASSED, NOT GOOD ENOUGH

67

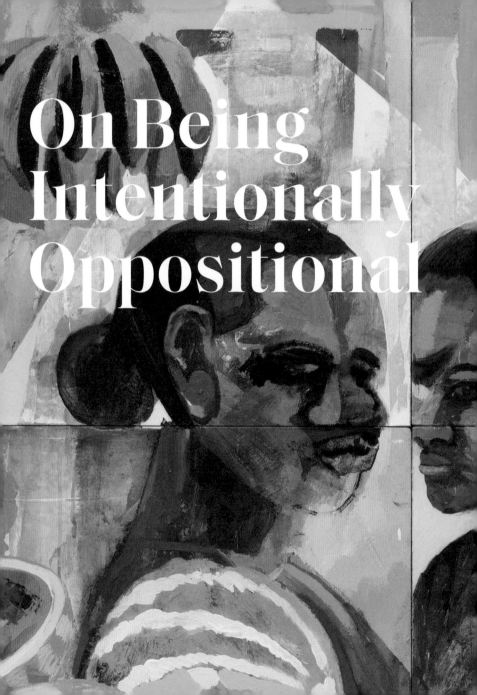

On Being Intentionally Oppositional

n my field of design, we are often expected to be positive, optimistic, and have good vibes as we move toward finding a solution. And while we have just explored how leaning into joy can be a valuable approach to design, sometimes being critical and even oppositional is the way to find and make social change.

An oppositional stance is characterized by resistance and dissent. You can be oppositional in different ways: in conversation, in how you read and research a situation, and in how you view and see the issue.

In one of the most widely used college composition texts in the United States, *They Say, I Say*, authors Gerald Graff and Cathy Birkenstein, professors at the University of Illinois–Chicago, emphasize the importance of being in conversation with the ideas of other people. To do this effectively, you have to recall what other people have said and then respond with your own opinion or ideas. This is an important skill when taking an oppositional stance. In stirring up change, we must notice the ideas of others, recall and recap those ideas, then react to them with our own ideas. Our response can be critical or take an opposing view, and in that dialogue we can come to a deeper understanding of the original idea.

In her essay "The Oppositional Gaze: Black Female Spectators," the author bell hooks describes staring at adults as a child and acknowledging the power of looking, even though as a child she was in a subordinate role. The oppositional gaze is intentionally critical of the dominant culture. hooks emphasizes the agency of looking at something from an oppositional viewpoint, giving a seemingly passive role more power and agency. The agency comes through making the world around you react to the opposition that they see in your eyes.

Having an oppositional perspective means that you will *intentionally* not read the world through the dominant point of view when designing change. Dominant interpretations favor the dominant group that will benefit from that perspective, such as cisgender white nondisabled men.

Oppositional interpretations *intentionally* reject the dominant view and make meaning through alternative lenses. Interpreting the world around us through an oppositional lens helps us to perceive themes and messages that might be missed entirely when viewed through the dominant lens. The oppositional lens reveals unintended consequences and harm that might affect people outside the dominant group.

You can lean into your own positionality to find that oppositional lens. Think back to the positionality statement that you made at the start of this book. Which of your historically excluded identities are not represented by the dominant group? This may be your race or ethnicity, gender, ability status, or another element of your identity. How does the issue change when read specifically through that lens?

Readings of the world from diverse perspectives and worldviews will uncover different themes. An underrepresented minority group may read a message differently than what was intended by the creator of the message. For instance, Black Twitter, an informal community of Black users on Twitter, was an excellent place to find oppositional views of the world around us through a Black lens. Black Twitter highlighted Black perspectives on diversity in TV, politics, media faux pas, and more.

A queer oppositional reading of the world may highlight instances of oppressive heteronormativity—such as assumptions that everyone is straight—or this lens may also highlight unnecessary gender binaries. A feminist oppositional stance will uncover sexism and the objectification of women. There are other oppositional lenses beyond race, gender, and sexuality. For example, as a mother, I find myself reading events through a maternal oppositional lens. When a colleague schedules meetings at 7 p.m., for example, it might tell me that he doesn't recognize my condition as a caregiver and the head of my family.

Oppositionality has agency, whether through oppositional reading and interpretation of the world or through gazing at the world through the lens of opposition. One form of agency is making the world react to your oppositionality. You could make them uncomfortable just through a side-eye, a bad look, letting them know that you see and you do not approve. Their discomfort will stir up change.

The other form of agency through oppositionality is more proactive and freeing. As your oppositionality reveals what must not continue, it makes space for you to dream and create the world that we need. An example of this comes from hooks, who wrote about Black women filmmakers who began to make films based on their opposition to how women were depicted in movies. Remember your power and agency in dreaming, making, and creating the world you want to see.

A Note on Taking an Oppositional Stance

Positions that oppose dominant messages are needed, but these positions can be exhausting. If this is your stance, you'll also need to create ways to rest, whether by completely switching off for a moment or throwing yourself into cooking or another form of creative practice, such as painting or poetry. Other options are making exercise a regular habit; this can be as simple as taking long walks outdoors. The skill of reading against the grain takes a lot of energy, so you need to find ways to consciously recharge, rest, and take care of yourself.

Your Turn

Using Opposition

Using an oppositional point of view will reveal greater complexity in all issues. When I teach about sustainability and design, I often use an oppositional lens, since the dominant reading of sustainability seems to cater to the middle and upper classes. This lens helped me see issues around race, economics, transportation, and other complex issues that impacted people who did not seem to have sustainable lifestyles. Here are some tips on how to use this viewpoint.

Find an article about a divisive contemporary issue. For example, single-use plastics.

- What is the dominant reading of the issue? It might be that single-use plastics are awful and the people who use them are evil.

- What is an oppositional reading of the issue? It might be that some people who need to use single-use plastics can't afford to buy multiple-use bags or they travel by public transport, making it harder to carry the extra load.

- What lens will you use in order to have an oppositional point of view? Here are some: race and ethnicity, gender, ability, class, or economic status.

After you've read the issue with an oppositional point of view, here are some reflection questions:

- Does your reading of the world align with the dominant reading, an oppositional reading, or something in between?

- Can you intentionally reject your perspectives and understand this issue from another point of view?

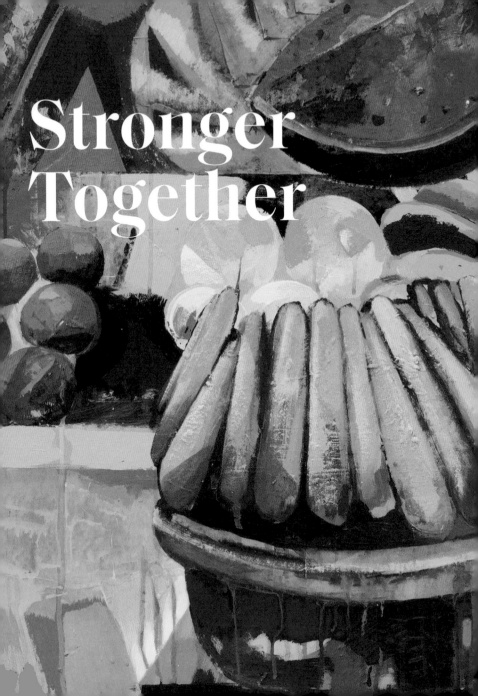

Stronger
Together

The path to change often starts with your own small individual actions: You can be kind to people. You can volunteer. You can support specific types of business. These small acts make change and can be the starting point of wider, more impactful social change. But to make lasting change, you need to join with others—only then can your little efforts come together and create significant and lasting impacts. Real change happens in community with others.

I would like you to focus on being in relationship with others and creating communities around you to help you stir up change. Relationships are your lifelines. They will offer you support and critical feedback and will be partners in making change.

The concept of relationality states that we are inter-connected and live in relation to others. While modern life emphasizes individuality and rewards individual efforts, it's also important that you make space for other people in your professional and personal lives to support you on your change-making journey. In this way, you will build communities around the work that you do and the change you would like to see and make.

We need both like-minded souls and dissenting voices around us to stir up change. As you build communities around you of like-minded souls, they will become your team, your support, and your mentors, the people who will carry you through hard times. When you have moments of self-doubt and imposter syndrome, you can reach out to your team and check the validity of your work.

Your like-minded souls may be your classmates. They may come from your wider network. They may be childhood friends. They may be colleagues from professional organizations. These people think like you. They'll help you manage your own self-doubts. They are essential to your success and well-being. And of course, you in turn can be the like-minded soul for others who may also need your support through difficult moments.

In my professional life, I've been "the only one" many times—the only Black woman at a predominantly white institution, the only designer in an art program, the only designer in a social innovation program, the only foreigner, and so on. Communities of people who were more like me helped support me when I felt alone. When I was a student in Brazil, all the Black and international students sat together at lunch. While at another university, I found support in affinity groups for Black students, staff, and faculty, and in my friendships with Latinx and Asian colleagues, since I was the only Black person there. Professionally, my colleagues at the Design Research

Society have buoyed me and validated my thought and scholarship, even when I was unsure of my practice. Even within the Design Research Society, I'm also part of a group of design researchers who focus on issues related to design in the Global South. Find and create community support for your journey, too.

Similarly, you also need some dissenting voices who won't agree with everything you do, to help keep you accountable and honest. Making good use of these dissenting voices will help deepen your work. They will make you do more research. They will make your work and how you defend it much more multidimensional. You can also follow these people from afar if you don't want them too close. There are a few academics whom I consider dissenting voices; I read and follow them from afar. As I write, I anticipate their comments on my work. The peer-review process in academia, where we get blind feedback from people who will not necessarily agree with our work, also serves this kind of purpose. This critical feedback helps keep us on track and focused on the impact we want our work to make.

Codesign

Codesign is an approach to designing *with* people rather than designing *for* people. It is about elevating the voices and knowledge of people with *lived* experience and combining that group with people with *learned* experience. In codesign, everybody has knowledge. And we all bring this knowledge together to mix it all up, to learn together. In this process, it's not the designer who has the knowledge and the design expertise. We respect that there are many different types of expertise within the group of people working together. In codesign, these different experiences work together to improve something that everyone cares about.

Cocreation can help us see equity gaps more clearly as we work with others. It helps us build on the dreams of others and go even further. In some codesign examples, collaborators lead the process; in others, they enrich the process through participation. Regardless, the aim is to innovate around the needs of people impacted by the issue.

Cocreation results in greater participation and brings the beneficiaries of the design into the action of solving their problems. If you are involved in civic innovation, cocreation also moves people up the ladder of citizen participation and helps people move from being passive to active citizens (a concept created by Sherry Arnstein). This approach can create greater buy-in, as people who may be skeptical about a process can be brought into the problem through the framing, brainstorming, and feedback phases. For example, in one workshop in New Orleans, police and residents came together to brainstorm ways that could improve the relationship between the two groups. Some citizens questioned the police and their motivations. By working collaboratively, the police were able to see that the residents wanted them to occupy different and more nurturing roles. Residents were also able to see the police officers as individuals and to understand some of the issues that influenced their work. The collaboration led to the proposal of new ideas and programs for the police.

Codesign is very much about prioritizing process over results. Results are important, but not more important than the process. Codesign processes move organically and at their own pace. You may plan the process, but the outcome will be difficult to predict and may not look like anything you would expect, since collaboration with other people will change what you're working together to do.

The Key Principles of Codesign

As designers focus more on social good and making change, they need to use methods that are compatible with activism, social justice, and collective good. Codesign is one of these design methods. It goes beyond cocreation, which is just about creating with affected stakeholders; it ensures collaboration with people who are affected by an issue throughout the entire design process. Here are four key principles of codesign.

Sharing Power. In the codesign process, one way to share power is by decentering the perspective of the lead designer and creating alternatives and choices for collaborators to select within the design process. Even more power is shifted if the alternatives are cocreated with the collaborators, or if the collaborators create all the options.

Prioritizing and Building Relationships. It is impossible for people to collaborate without first building trust and relationships. In stirring up change, relationships with others help move the process along. Sometimes we need food, drink, music, dance, and storytelling to create the right environment for collaboration. Codesign demands trust and safety so people can clearly voice their opinions, propose ideas that may seem ridiculous at first, and work together to propose solutions to the problems they have identified. Codesign draws on empathetic relationship-building with people who think like us, people who disagree with us, and people who will create with us.

Building Design Capability. In good codesign, each participant needs to tap into their design capabilities. Both people who consider themselves experts and people who consider themselves novices must be aware of their own skills and the skills of their collaborators. The more opportunities people have to practice a range of design abilities together—such as problem framing, brainstorming, and prototyping—the better the design capabilities of the entire team.

In the codesign process, we must ensure there is space and support for other people to participate in ways they might not have considered before.

Going Slowly. Codesign is a slow design process; this might also require new skills from everyone in the process, as many of us are typically expected to think and work more quickly. In codesign, sometimes it's important to remember the process takes the time that it takes, but if we prioritize sharing power, building relationships, and building design capability, this can certainly make the codesign process move more smoothly.

What Communities Support You?

Relationships with others are essential for creating change. Think about the community that supports you. Who are the like-minded souls, the dissenting voices, and the people with whom you will make change? Who can you codesign with? Consider these questions:

- What communities are you a part of?

- Do you have relationships with the three groups that were mentioned: like-minded people, people who will disagree with you, and people to make change with?

- How can you reach out to build communities around you?

- How can you slow down to honor the relationship-building process?

Create a map of these communities. Where do they overlap? What are the issues that are important to them?

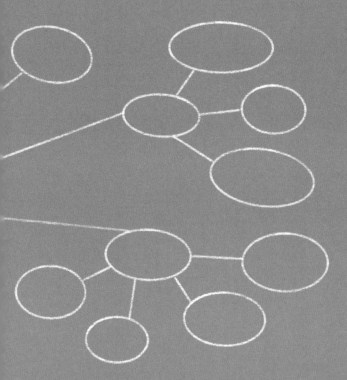

What World Do You Want to Design?

Envisioning Equitable Futures

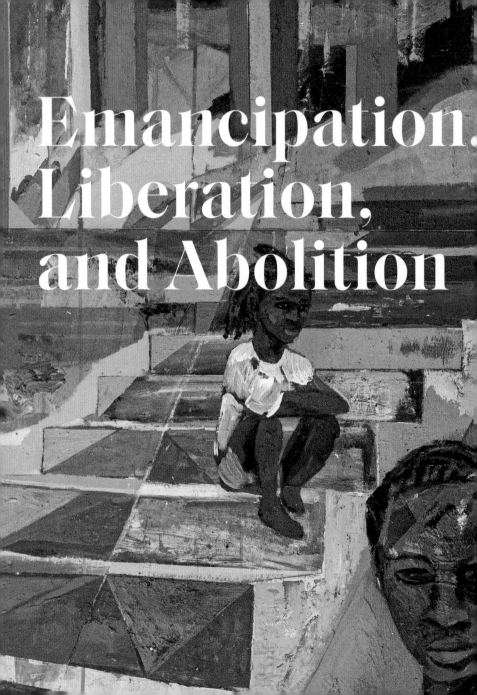

Emancipation, Liberation, and Abolition

E mancipation, *liberation*, and *abolition* are three words used to describe the end of chattel slavery in the Americas. Slavery was abolished in the Americas on different dates, ranging from as early as 1829, in Mexico, to as late as 1888, in Brazil. Emancipation proclamations led to the liberation of enslaved Africans throughout the Americas.

Emancipation, liberation, and abolition can also be used as principles to guide the design process. Sometimes we make progress through incremental change; other times we need to be more radical and abolish systems altogether, and that is where these principles can guide the design process. Reform and incremental change are both an approach to change that is built on tweaking older designs and systems. Supposedly reform is easier to achieve than radical change, and in modern times, abolition and reform are regularly juxtaposed. But sometimes abolition is the only solution. What if the abolitionists were merely seeking a less abominable form of slavery? No! Thank goodness they sought to end the abominable system. Incrementally changing what is fundamentally wrong just perpetuates unfair systems.

As you work to change the world, keep the lessons of emancipation, liberation, and abolition in your toolkit.

Emancipation

When I think about emancipation, two quotes come to mind. The first is a West African proverb: "Until the lion has his or her own storyteller, the hunter will always have the best part of the story." The second is from a 1983 speech by Ed Roberts to members of the disability movement, which echoed lessons from the civil rights movement: "When others speak for you, you lose." Here's what I'm getting at: what differentiates an emancipatory approach to design from a nonemancipatory one is that the former insists that people impacted by the issue speak for themselves.

In design, using an emancipatory approach means that marginalized people drive the design and research process. This approach requires designers to decenter people who would normally have more power—such as company executives, city officials, and even the design team—and to understand and center the issues of the people impacted by the problem area.

An emancipatory approach to design starts at the very beginning, with the research phase. In emancipatory research, questions and agendas are driven by the people who are most impacted by this research. In disability studies, this means that people with disabilities have greater control over research agendas than academics, members of the medical community, or public officials.

Centering the voices, needs, and perspectives of people who are directly affected by issues ensures that these issues are framed appropriately. An emancipatory approach entails redistributing power away from where it traditionally lies—with the elite researcher or government official. An emancipatory approach confronts social oppression by redistributing power to those who would not usually have held it. It facilitates the uncovering and reframing of issues that would be missed through the lens of the dominant group.

Liberation

Liberation is defined as social, cultural, economic, and political freedom and emancipation to have agency, control, and power over one's life. To live life freely, unaffected and unharmed by conditions of oppression, is to experience liberation.

Liberation is the act of setting someone free from imprisonment, slavery, or oppression; it is release. It is also freedom from limits on thought or behavior. According to Paulo Freire, we become liberated as we reflect on the world and recognize that we have the power to take action and transform it. Understanding both the dynamics of oppression and one's agency in making change contributes to a liberatory consciousness.

Here are two examples of how a liberatory consciousness can set you free. My friend Nii in South Africa is a design professor. He shared a liberatory moment when his students and graduates stopped looking for jobs and recognized that they could create their own businesses to employ themselves and other people. In this way they could begin to move beyond the barriers that held them back. Being their own bosses freed up their design practice so they could concentrate on the impact they wanted to create rather than the demands of their employers.

Another example is from design research I did with children in a rural village in Trinidad. The aim of the design curriculum that I created for this research was to build a liberatory consciousness for the students through design. The children, who ranged in age from nine to twelve, were encouraged to reflect on their lives, school, and village. Their liberatory awareness was fostered as we discussed how they could, as individuals and in groups, design responses to the forces that were limiting them and preventing them from achieving their potential. They designed events to make people see their village, services to clean up the litter, apps to connect people. As we designed the solutions together, they learned about their own agency.

Your Turn

Building an Abolitionary Mindset

In the nineteenth century, abolitionists worked hard to end almost 250 years of chattel slavery in the British colonies and the United States. We can connect design to the abolition of slavery in two ways. Designed artifacts were used to get the message out about the harsh realities of slavery through pamphlets, leaflets, slogans, illustrated children's books, and Wedgewood coins. Other creative platforms such as paintings by famous artists, music, and sermons also played a role in creating a greater awareness about the evils of slavery. The second role of these creative artifacts was to facilitate ways to imagine alternative possibilities. We can draw on these two aims in present times as we use abolition as a guiding principle in creating change.

- How can you use design and creativity to create greater awareness of the need for change?

- How can you use these methods to help people envision something new?

Reflect on the change you're trying to make and see how you can respond to these questions.

Shifting Power

Emancipation and liberation require major power shifts. In the emancipation and liberation process, people become free and can no longer be controlled. In emancipatory work, power and agency shift to the people who are impacted. The following activity was built around *empowerment*, a much-overused but essential word for an essential step on the journey to equity-centeredness. By consciously reflecting on how your work will shift power, you will be able to see more clearly if your work promotes people's empowerment.

Challenge yourself to think of a moment when you heard of people being empowered. For people to be empowered, power must be moved from one place to another. In that moment, how did the power move? Where did the power shift happen?

Now think of your own work and interest in social change. How will you shift power in this work? Who will you shift the power to?

My _____
[THE KIND OF WORK YOU DO]

work shifts power _____
[FROM WHOM TO WHOM]

by _____
[HOW YOUR WORK SHIFTS POWER]

Here are some post-design reflection questions to ask yourself:

- Where and how did power shift in the project?

- How will my work contribute to stopping oppression?

- What is my own potential to cause harm through my work?

- How am I also oppressing through this work?

Abolition

Abolition is the act of abolishing a system, practice, or institution. Abolition is a word that I'm now bringing into all my design conversations. I have adopted abolition as a design principle to promote radical change. I weave this principle into the brainstorming part of my design classes. For me, it is necessary to think about abolition as a design principle so that we can create a space where we can talk about getting rid of systems that absolutely do not work. I fear that incremental change is not disruptive enough. Sometimes we must intentionally create spaces to consider what we must simply abolish.

The focus on abolition can help us to see unfair practices. For me, entrance exams and standardized tests need to be abolished. I don't have an alternative yet, and paradoxically I work for a regional examining body in the Caribbean. But clearly identifying what needs to be abolished can help me visualize a range of practices and ground my philosophy as I create options.

Use an abolitionary mindset to find where radical change is needed and where incremental change may just be propping up old, exclusive, and problematic systems. In researching this book, I discovered that the high school entrance exam in Trinidad still used today is built on the College Entrance Exam created in 1941. This exam was created so that the colony of Trinidad had a small elite intellectual class. The exam has received only incremental changes over the last eighty years. It is time for a more radical approach. What could change look like if we abolish it completely?

What other broken systems exist today? Education? Healthcare? Mass incarceration? Law enforcement? What institutions and systems cause harm? What would variations of these systems look like if, instead of causing harm, they were based on more nurturing principles such as care, healing, stewardship? What are the systems that just need to be abolished? Abolition as a design principle can help you ultimately reframe the way you ask these questions. What do you have to abolish to ensure that you get to the fairness you want?

Think Like an Abolitionist

In design workshops, design researcher Hannah Korsmeyer often encourages designers to move beyond a mindset of fixing and solving. Thinking in an abolitionist way is one way to move beyond this fixing frame. Though designers like to "fix" problems, this illustration offers design principles that provide alternatives to a fixing mindset and that should be incompatible with harm. Consider broken systems around you and reflect how they can be reframed around these principles.

These are principles from my Good Vibes Alphabet, which intentionally focuses on positive design principles for social change.

Abolition

How can the system be completely abolished? What was the broken system trying to address? What will be the focus of the new system?

Buen vivir

Can the new system promote a life of dignity, plenitude, balance, and harmony?

Care

Can the new system promote a culture of care by ensuring that people thrive and feel seen and valued?

Interdependence

How can the new system foster interdependence?

Joy

What brings joy to people in the broken system? Can the new system build on joy?

Kin

Can the new system build relationships within families rather than break these relationships? Can the new system foster kinship?

Liberation

How can the new system support the collective liberation of all of the actors within the it?

Relationality

How will the new system build relationships between people within the system?

Well-being

How can the new system promote the positive well-being of the people who use it?

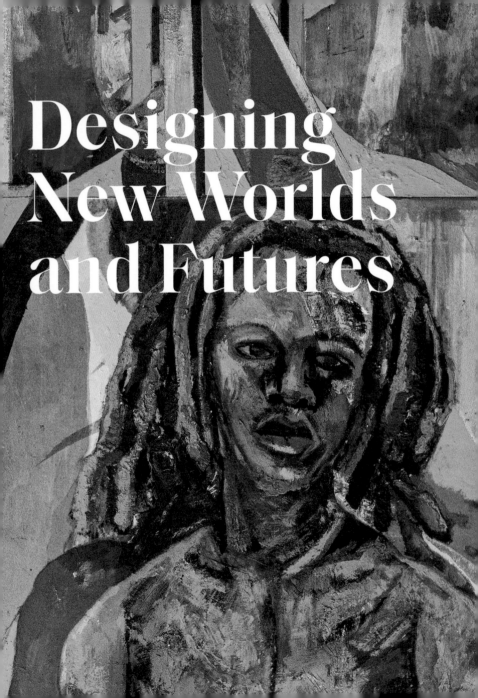

Designing
New Worlds
and Futures

esign is an act of world creation. And the world-building quality of design is one reason why design can lead change—and why you're reading a book on change by a designer! The Nobel laureate and computer scientist Herbert Simon defined design as changing existing situations to preferred ones. If we are designing for the future, shouldn't we also seek to change it simultaneously? Your interest in making futures is exactly why you need to see what is wrong with the present as you build. You can focus every design question on equity and social justice by asking: How might we change existing situations into preferred and more equitable ones where everyone will enjoy full and healthy lives in the future?

For several years, I adapted a method called Critical Utopian Action Research (CUAR) to spark critical conversations about social change. This method begins with participants being critical of a current situation. To start, we talk about everything that is wrong with the issue and freely critique the problem. Next, we dream of where we want to go and the future we want to see. Finally, the design question turns to *how* we will get to the future that we want. These are the questions that designers ask all the time. This is a codesign process about building new futures where participants can dream together of the desired state and create action to get there.

This process is useful because it gives oppressed people space to dream where they might otherwise not have been able to—because they weren't focused at the time, because they have to hustle, or because they have to battle with other people's preconceived notions of them. This process allows people to bring their own expertise and lived experience to discussions on change and their own cultural experiences to the actual design activities. It gives people the space to be critical of their circumstances and to start thinking about a better way. This opens everyone up to move to action through design.

I've used this simple method in many workshops and with different audiences. From the children in rural Trinidad who critiqued their school and their village to students in Puerto Rico (with Dr. Maria de Mater O'Neill) imagining a post–Hurricane Maria Puerto Rico, from teenage boys in Oakland imagining how they could change their worlds with superpowers and technology to residents of New Orleans trying to imagine a different public health experience, given what they had experienced in the pandemic.

Changing the world must start with recognizing that something is not right, then allowing space to dream of what the "right" thing could be, and finally making a plan for achieving it. All oppressed people are dreaming, plotting, scheming, designing, and imagining the change they want. This process embraces that.

Since I started my work with CUAR, I've become very interested in utopia, Afrofuturism, and other themes related to speculation and futures and have started combining these with my equity-focused work. For me, combining equity and a focus on the future creates a more visionary and liberatory way of framing equity, because it creates space for discussion and dreaming about radical change. Sometimes equity work can focus too much on the people who are doing the oppressing and supporting them on their journey toward change, or it can focus too much on the victimhood of people who face oppression. Bringing in the future lens creates more agency, as people can collaborate to build the futures they want.

A focus on utopia opens up the frame for people to dream and imagine without the constraints of the current times. People from underrepresented minorities and oppressed groups—such as Black and indigenous people, women, and LGBTQ+ communities—need imaginative frames to envision futures where they are not oppressed and constrained in the ways they are in the present. Part of the act of liberation is recognizing that one's oppression is not a perpetual state and transformation is possible.

People can sometimes be unimaginative about closing equity gaps when we design for the present or the near future. As we imagine our futures, I like to push people into the far future. I've set design briefs in 2054, 2072, even the year 2100. Forcing people into the far-distant future helps them imagine futures without barriers. People can easily think change is too radical, but considering much further out makes the radical seem less extreme.

Others have done this before me. I want to believe that antislavery abolitionists, for example, were futurists who knew that slavery was wrong, knew where they wanted to go, and figured out how to get there. The abolitionist painter William Blake exemplified this critical utopian futurism. In the 1790s, Blake created a radical vision for a post-slavery world through his art. Antislavery abolitionists must have imagined a radical future that led to change. We did it before, and we can do it again.

When dreaming about the future, it's also valuable to dream with others. We don't make change by ourselves.

A focus on utopia opens
up the frame for people to
dream and imagine without
the constraints of the
current times.

Words That Express a World of Many Worlds

As you work in the arena of world-changing, you'll come across many concepts that overlap and are often confused.

Antihegemony is working against or dismantling the status quo or the power of a dominant force.

Antiracism is a stance of actively opposing racism.

Decolonization is the undoing of colonialism.

Diversity, equity, and inclusion (DEI) promotes greater participation of underrepresented or nondominant individuals or groups in a space that is dominated by one group.

Pluriversality envisions a world in which many worlds coexist at the same time.

All of these concepts share the pushback against a single story, a one-world world. We inhabit many worlds at the same time, and we can keep that in mind as we stir up change.

All of these concepts also point to a question: How might we create different worlds beyond the dominant culture? How might we create an antiracist world? How might we create more diversity, equity, and inclusion in the world? How might we undo the impact of colonialism? Learn these concepts and have them fuel the questions in your work. Keep thinking about how you can create change in these areas by continually creating a "how might we" statement. Use this fill-in-the-blank prompt as a start.

How might we _____
[GO WHERE WE WANT TO GO; THAT IS, DESCRIBE UTOPIA]

and not end up _____
[DESCRIBE THE STATE THAT WE DO NOT WANT]

Example: How might we turn Belmont into a center for music innovation and creativity, and not end up with a gentrified neighborhood where long-time residents no longer feel welcome?

The Pluriverse: One World, Many Worlds

In creating and imagining new worlds, we must not forget that, as decolonial theorists Marisol de la Cadena and Mario Blaser say, we live in a world of many worlds. Even though the dominant worldview is male, Euro-American, and cisgendered straight, a helpful exercise is to imagine many different points of view in the future. Straight white men need not dominate the future. How would the future change if we focused on dominance by different groups? What are the many worlds and futures that we can create in the future?

The concept of a pluriverse was created by the Zapatistas, a group of mainly indigenous activists from southern Mexico. It refers to a world in which many worlds fit.

I first heard Arturo Escobar use the term *pluriverse* in 2018. He was articulating what I had been thinking. He showed the radical difference in the kinds of questions that interested the designers of the Global North and the Global South. Though we were part of the same profession, we occupied different worlds. The word *pluriverse* resonated with me and the work that I was doing.

Universe means "the whole world, cosmos, the totality of existing things"; it's from Latin *universum*, meaning "all things, everybody, all people, the whole world." The pluriverse conjures up an image of many worlds turning at the same time. Some of these worlds will connect and some won't, but they all exist simultaneously.

My interest in the pluriverse has been about recognizing that there are many worlds and different ways of being, knowing, and doing. My interest in pluriversal design is about sharing stories and practices from the many worlds or universes of design and learning together with people from other worlds. My interest was always more about what I could learn from Indian design practice, Colombian design practice, Kenyan design practice, and so on, and what I could bring back to my teaching in Trinidad and later on to my teaching and practice in North America. How could I use experiences from the pluriverse to create change?

What is going on in other worlds regarding the change you want to see? What are other questions, approaches, strategies, practices? Different questions will be central in different worlds. You need the skill of listening to these different points of view and understanding how these new questions can make life better across all the worlds. How can you recognize and celebrate the change-making practices of people around the world? What does that change mean in different parts of the pluriverse? What do the many worlds or universes of change look like?

Freire said that "we did not come into this world to keep it as it is. Our challenge is to remake the world. We have to change it." So the closing challenge for this section is to make the change that is needed in the worlds in which you live.

Your Turn

World Building

One of your superpowers as an artist and designer is your ability to really see and imagine that which does not yet exist—to reimagine the world and create new beginnings. You can use that ability to create hope where others find none. You can help others dream of new and different worlds, free of the problems and constraints of today, and play a role in making these dreams real. I have described Critical Utopian Action Research. Here's an activity to help you understand how to use this method.

CUAR connects critiques with utopian ideas and actions. Gather together a group of people to brainstorm about an issue that you would like to address. This group could be children or adults, family members or students in a class, and so on. Explain the method to the group: You will first critique, then dream, then chart a path.

WHAT IS WRONG?

HOW WILL WE GET THERE?

WHERE DO WE WANT TO GO?

What Is Wrong?

1 Use prompts to have critical discussion about the issue. I have used the United Declaration of Human Rights, The Sustainable Development Goals, and The Rights of the Child as starting points for discussion. I have also used articles and stories in the media presenting both sides of an argument to get the conversation started.

2 Ensure that you have created a space or environment where people can be freely and openly critical of an issue without fear of repercussions.

3 Brainstorm around all that is wrong within the issue of focus. Some people might want to focus on issues within the scope or sphere of control of the people doing the brainstorming. Personally, I prefer to just brain dump about everything that is wrong. Sometimes I'll use a question format, like "Why can't homeless people sleep in empty hotels?" Other times I'll use a sentence format, like "People ignoring homeless people is a problem." There are no right answers. The aim of this activity is to have people think about and critically discuss the area of focus.

Like the reflection on positionality, the "what is wrong?" space can bring up uncomfortable feelings that must be acknowledged. In Portuguese, my second language, the words for grief and fight are so close: *luto* means "grief, sorrow, mourning, or lamentation," while *luta* means "fight or struggle." People may feel grief as part of the process of moving toward creating social change, as they reflect on what is missed and what has been denied to them, or even when they reflect on how far there is to go before reaching their goal. It is important to recognize these feelings.

The slogan *A luta continua* ("the struggle continues") was the rallying cry of the FRELIMO movement in Mozambique. It is known widely by many people who know very little about Mozambique and its freedom struggle in the 1960s and '70s. But most don't recall the second part of the phrase, *vitoria é certa.* ("victory is certain"). In the struggle for social change, this is comforting to keep in mind.

Where Do We Want to Go?

This is the fun part, where we imagine the worlds we want to create. However, it can take an infusion of energy for some groups to get them into the dreamspace. They have lost sight of their own agency. They feel hopeless. They think it is futile to dream of new possibilities when change is unlikely to happen. This is where you need to be a peppy cheerleader and infuse the group with optimism. I can be over-the-top and theatrical in this phase. I'll wear a costume with a cape. I'll play music from superhero movies. I'll set a mood with props that transport us into the future. I'll encourage people to have fun dreaming.

Encourage people to describe the future they want with regard to the issue in focus. They can be playful or realistic, but they must imagine what a thriving future looks like. You can use prompts to help them get there. Give them a year that's several years away. I like to think of what the world will be like at my hundredth birthday, for example. I sometimes ask people to finish the sentence

"In the year . . . there will be no more . . ." or "In the year . . . there will only be . . ." This can lead to radical ideas. My students have replied with ideas like these:

- In 2050 there will only be small businesses.
- In 2050 those who teach our children will have extensive mental health training.
- In 2050 college will be free.

For this phase, the focus is on *what*: What is the future we want?

How Will We Get There?

How is a designing and building word. This is the phase in which we design with others and make plans to get to the futures we want. Here's where we build the worlds that we want and need. This phase involves envisioning both the solution and the details of the solution.

1 With your group, brainstorm about how problems could be addressed. What could solutions look like?

2 Ask people to think of the *how* within different scopes. For example, what is an immediate or short-term *how* or a small step toward the goal? What is a long-term or bigger step that would take more work and effort to achieve?

3 Think about the details needed to implement a few of the ideas. What types of plans are needed for either the short or the long term? Who needs to be engaged to make the plan successful?

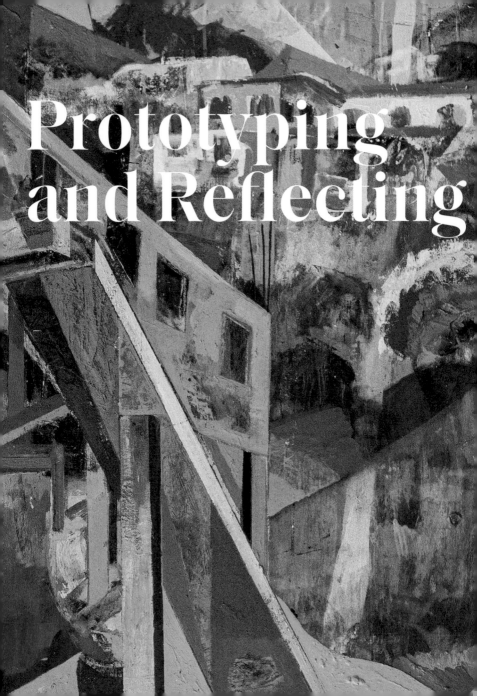

Prototyping and Reflecting

W hat do you want to change? What idea can you prototype and share to push your movement forward? In stirring up change, there should be some urgency— share your ideas and prototypes early and often for feedback. You can use this approach for physical objects, for essays, for policies, programs, relationships, classes, food—in short, for anything. Will you write an article to share your solution? A letter to the editor? Will you approach your mayor or your school to ask them to try out your solution? Whatever you create does not have to be perfect when sharing it. Don't wait until the idea is perfect. Yours might be the spark to get things going.

Wearing one of my many hats, I have worked with organizations that support cities and agencies like police departments and public utility companies. In this work we focus on social innovation and have explored many themes, including public safety, violence, litter, public utilities like water, and the relationship between the residents and the police. Our prototypes have looked different for each project.

In the work between the police and residents, residents wanted to see the police as less threatening and adopting more caretaking and relationship-building roles in society, such as being more involved in afterschool programs and youth development. The prototypes included rough hand-built models and role-play that demonstrated what improved relationships could look like. They even prototyped fun ideas like police-led community fitness classes for the elderly, a movie night, and an ice cream truck. Sometimes the ideas in the prototypes may border on the absurd or the ridiculous, but they help people express themselves and move toward ideas that are more concrete. The models helped people start to think about how to operationalize ideas, while the role play depicted the emotions that people wanted in the new experiences.

Your prototype about social change can do and be many things. It can help you galvanize support for your cause. It can provide proof of concept and be a mini-test for others. It can help you work out the logistics of your idea.

Prototyping Change

A prototype is a great way to test your ideas. Think about the issue you would like to focus on. Here are some reflection questions to help you create some focus.

- What needs to change?
- What's your vision for change?
- Who needs to be involved?
- Who needs to give feedback?
- What emotional change are you trying to create for the people affected by the issue?

Prototyping Action

Think about your vision for change in the questions above, then consider the following questions.

- How can you get to that vision?
- What might be a perfect version of your solution if there were no limits on resources?
- How can you galvanize other people around the cause?

Now bring that back to the present:

- Can you make a very rough version of your solution?
- Is there a much simpler way of achieving the same outcome as by using the perfect solution?
- Who can you share this idea with?
- How can you get the word out?

Reflecting

Both design and creating change are based in action—through connecting with people, trying things out, and iterative prototyping. And while all this doing is important, it is only by reflecting that you can see the value of your actions. You must also pause and learn from what you have done. Stopping to reflect will help to make you aware of what you might have missed and think of who else should have been involved in the conversation.

Sociologist Jack Mezirow, inspired by Paulo Freire, believed that critical reflection was an essential component of transformation, specifically Transformative Learning for adults, a learning theory where meaning is created through reflection and dialogue, which leads to radical shifts in perspective. According to Mezirow, we can change our perspective and transform our worldview, we can change some of our assumptions and beliefs, and we can gain a new understanding of the world—all through critical reflection. Combining critical reflection with the action and agency of design can improve your outcomes.

Reflecting on change (or on prototypes for ideas that we want to implement to cause change) can also help us see how we can create more significant impact. When reflecting, you can have two points of view—reflecting on both what went wrong and what went well—and use both to grow.

I have referred to Paulo Freire many times throughout this book. Another of his key ideas is learning to find or pose problems instead of solving them. Problem posing rather than problem solving acknowledges that "it" is not finished. While designers are trained to "solve" problems, in problem posing we redefine existing problems and ask new questions.

Problem solving suggests an unrealistic state of completion in the face of problems that can't be simply resolved. "Wicked problems," such as homelessness, poverty, and sustainability, are considered impossible to solve. Reflection creates space for us to explore what new questions we need to focus on to address such complex issues.

By intentionally taking the time to stop and think about the people you collaborate with, even your adversaries, you'll be able to understand the viewpoint of others and even to change your own perspective. In this way, critical reflection on ourselves, our relationships, and our interactions with others humanizes us and is part of our collective liberation.

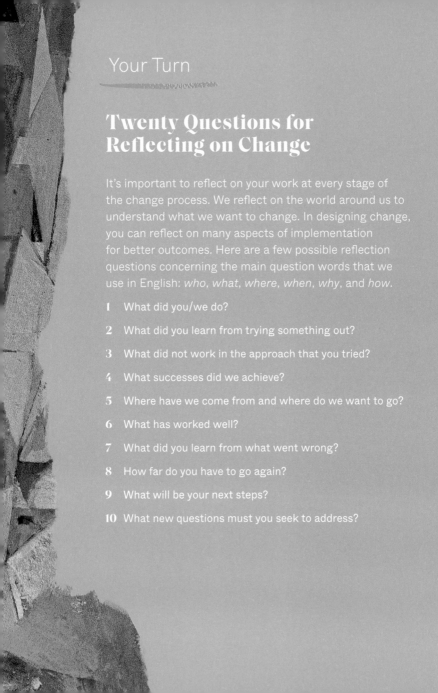

Your Turn

Twenty Questions for Reflecting on Change

It's important to reflect on your work at every stage of the change process. We reflect on the world around us to understand what we want to change. In designing change, you can reflect on many aspects of implementation for better outcomes. Here are a few possible reflection questions concerning the main question words that we use in English: *who*, *what*, *where*, *when*, *why*, and *how*.

1   What did you/we do?

2   What did you learn from trying something out?

3   What did not work in the approach that you tried?

4   What successes did we achieve?

5   Where have we come from and where do we want to go?

6   What has worked well?

7   What did you learn from what went wrong?

8   How far do you have to go again?

9   What will be your next steps?

10   What new questions must you seek to address?

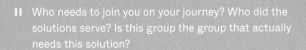

11 Who needs to join you on your journey? Who did the solutions serve? Is this group the group that actually needs this solution?

12 Who has power? Who is oppressed? Why?

13 Whose voice was missing from the process?

14 How does the solution work? What needs to be clearer now that you have tried something out?

15 Does your solution still focus on the goal of reducing oppression?

16 What could your solution look like through a different delivery mode?

17 What would you have done differently if you had to repeat the exercise?

18 What is a better way forward?

19 When can your solution can create the biggest impact?

20 What if . . . ?

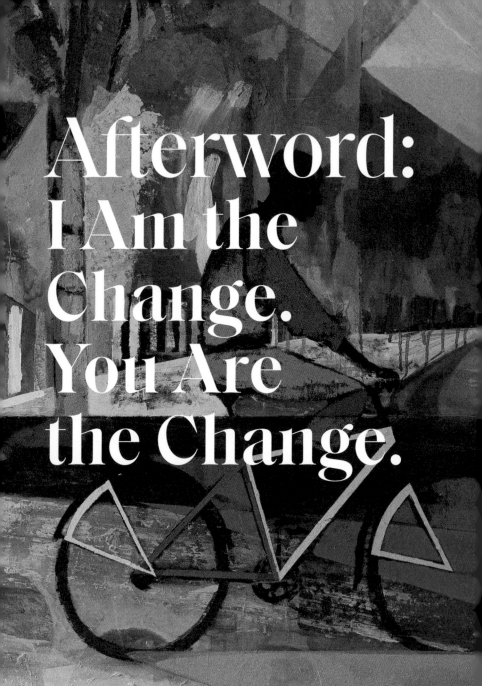

Afterword: I Am the Change. You Are the Change.

We may have different opinions about how to fix those inequities, but an acknowledgment of the inequities is essential to a productive conversation.

—Beverly Tatum

There is no single recipe for creating lasting social impact. We can't just download a recipe to follow step by step and then—ta-da!—we have equity and social change. Throughout this book, I have sought to share strategies that I've learned from years of reading, doing, and design practice that could be helpful in your quest for equity, thriving, social justice, and social change. Still, like the person who adapts a recipe to suit what they have available in their pantry, you're going to have to adjust these strategies to suit the problems you're addressing and the change you want to make.

One big idea that I'd like you to take away from the book is that to make change, you have to understand what oppression is, learn to see where it is happening, and identify real issues that are preventing people from leading full and thriving lives. In this first phase of the design for equity process, you can develop a laser focus on understanding what is wrong by learning to listen and see from many different points of view and focusing on equity and justice as you learn to question the world.

Once you understand the oppression and learn to see it, your emotional connections, your understanding of your own emotions, and the emotions of others all will support you through the process of making change. Take action by responding to emotions like anger and joy. Take action by building communities with others and moving together. Build relationships with people who will give you critical feedback on your work.

As you design your solutions, consider using alternative design principles such as abolition, liberation, emancipation, relationality, community—visionary design principles that will get you to the equitable futures we need. I want you to design your response to oppression. Design oppression out of products and services. Take action by envisioning futures where this oppression no longer exists, and design your way to these futures. We learn through action. So don't wait until your solutions and ideas are perfect. Put them out there so you can grow them with other people.

Then, after you've done your work, take time to reflect on what was successful, what could have gone better, and how your work impacts what you want to change. Is it a small impact, like helping your grandparent to understand new uses of pronouns, or a big impact, like getting your city council to adopt participatory governance strategies? Take comfort in knowing that even small steps move change forward. Critical reflection will help you see the impact of your work. It will help you understand the perspective of others, and it will provide opportunities to see new directions that can be taken.

Everyone who has read this book has gotten the same recipes and ingredients or the same information and activities, but what happens next depends on you. So *you* are an essential ingredient in the recipe. Your positionality affects what change you want to make and how you will go about it. Bring your authentic self to the change process. Dig deep into your positionality to see issues relevant to you and your community. Understand the complexity of your own identity. Reflect on your point of view. How is it similar to or different from that of others? Bring your true self to all your work. When you are being excluded or not represented, make your own spaces so that you and your point of view are not made invisible.

We need you to be you! Be unapologetically who you are! Add yourself as a key ingredient in whatever you do!

Go boldly and go confidently into the world. We have no idea yet of all the new and exciting change you are going to stir up. Go off and create paths and work that we never dreamed possible!

Recommendations for Further Reading

Here are some of my go-to readings to help me understand the issues that are related to making social change.

Feminism and Patriarchy

Ahmed, Sarah. *Living a Feminist Life*. Duke University Press, 2017.

Bagshaw, Joanne L. *The Feminist Handbook: Practical Tools to Resist Sexism and Dismantle the Patriarchy*. New Harbinger, 2019.

Eltahawy, Mona. *The Seven Necessary Sins for Women and Girls*. Beacon Press, 2019.

hooks, bell. *The Will to Change: Men, Masculinity, and Love*. Atria, 2003.

Decoloniality and Pluriversality

de la Cadena, Marisol, and Mario Blaser. *A World of Many Worlds*. Duke University Press, 2018.

de Sousa Santos, Boaventura. *Epistemologies of the South: Justice Against Epistemicide*. Routledge, 2014.

Escobar, Arturo. *Designs for the Pluriverse: Radical Interdependence, Autonomy, and the Making of Worlds*. Duke University Press, 2018.

Understanding Racism

Stauffer, Jason, "The Black Homeownership Gap Is Larger Than It Was 60 Years Ago. COVID-19 Made It Worse," NextAdvisor (April 21, 2022), https://time.com/nextadvisor/mortgages/what-is-black-homeownership-gap.

Tatum, Beverly. *Why Are All the Black Kids Sitting Together in the Cafeteria? And Other Conversations About Race.* Basic Books, 1997.

Change

brown, adrienne maree. *Holding Change: The Way of Emergent Strategy Facilitation and Mediation* (Emergent Strategy Series, 4). AK Press, 2021.

Freire, Paulo. *Pedagogy of Freedom: Ethics, Democracy, and Civic Courage.* Rowman & Littlefield, 1998.

Freire, Paulo. *Pedagogy of the Oppressed*, 50th anniversary 4th edition. Bloomsbury Academic, 2018.

hooks, bell. *Teaching Community: A Pedagogy of Hope.* Routledge, 2003.

hooks, bell. *Teaching to Transgress: Education as the Practice of Freedom.* Routledge, 1994.

Levins Morales, Aurora. *Medicine Stories: Essays for Radicals.* Duke University Press, 2019.

VanMuijen, Abby. "The Emotion Wheel." https://www.avanmuijen.com/watercolor-emotion-wheel

Acknowledgments

I would like to acknowledge the unbelievable support that I have received from my family. To my parents, Kenty and Sonia: Thank you for your open, supportive, and empowering parenting. Thank you for being brave enough to let me go down my own path at a young age. I only received encouragement from you, even though I'm sure you must have been scared or even skeptical. Thank you also for the many conversations as I was writing this book. You gave me great insights into pre-Independence life in the Caribbean and why we need to keep striving for equity. To my siblings, Adrienne and André, thank you for being there and being willing to just jump in and help with parenting and building our family memories. To my siblings' children, Sam and Anaïs, I hope that this book will inspire you to always fight for equity and justice. Finally, to my son, Azure, you are the main reason I am striving for equity. I hope your world is fairer than the one I grew up in.

I would also like to thank my friend Che Lovelace for allowing me to use his beautiful paintings to illustrate this book.

Index

Published in the United States by Ten Speed Press, an imprint of
Random House, a division of Penguin Random House LLC, New York.
TenSpeed.com

Ten Speed Press and the Ten Speed Press colophon are registered trademarks
of Penguin Random House LLC.

Image on page 67 reprinted with permission from Abby VanMuijen.

Typefaces: Hope Meng's d.sign, Dinamo's Whyte, Mostardesign's Archeron,
and Schick Toikka's Saol

Library of Congress Cataloging-in-Publication Data
Names: Noel, Lesley-Ann, author.
Title: Design Social Change : take action, work toward equity, and
    challenge the status quo / Lesley-Ann Noel ; artwork by Ché Lovelace.
Description: California : Ten Speed Press, [2023] | Includes index.
Identifiers: LCCN 2022045701 (print) | LCCN 2022045702 (ebook) |
    ISBN 9781984858146 (trade paperback) | ISBN 9781984858153 (ebook)
Subjects: LCSH: Social change. | Social participation. | Self-realization.
Classification: LCC HM831 .N64 2023 (print) | LCC HM831 (ebook) |
    DDC 303.4—dc23/eng/20220929
LC record available at https://lccn.loc.gov/2022045701
LC ebook record available at https://lccn.loc.gov/2022045702
Trade Paperback ISBN: 978-1-9848-5814-6
eBook ISBN: 978-1-9848-5815-3

Printed in China

Acquiring editor: Hannah Rahill | Project editor: Kim Keller
Production editor: Sohayla Farman
Designer: Emma Campion | Production designers: Mari Gill and Faith Hague
Production and prepress color manager: Jane Chinn
Copyeditor: Kristi Hein | Proofreader: Lisa Brousseau | Indexer: Ken DellaPenta
Publicist: Natalie Yera | Marketer: Chloe Aryeh
d.school creative team: Jenn Brown, Charlotte Burgess-Auburn, Scott Doorley

10 9 8 7 6 5 4 3 2 1

First Edition